CH00686894

The Amorous Prawn

A Comedy

Anthony Kimmins

SAMUEL FRENCH

FOUNDED 1830

SAMUELFRENCH-LONDON.CO.UK
SAMUELFRENCH.COM

ISBN 978-0-573-01018-7

www.samuelfrench-london.co.uk

www.samuelfrench.com

THE AMOROUS PRAWN

Produced at The Saville Theatre, London, on the 9th December 1959, with the following cast of characters:

(in the order of their appearance)

CORPORAL SYDNEY GREEN	*Stanley Baxter*
PRIVATE BIDDY O'HARA, W.R.A.C.	*Lucy Young*
PRIVATE SUZIE TIDMARSH, W.R.A.C.	*Jean Aubrey*
LADY FITZADAM	*Evelyn Laye*
MAJOR-GENERAL SIR HAMISH FITZADAM, K.B.E., C.B., D.S.O.	*Walter Fitzgerald*
PRIVATE ALBERT HUGGINS	*Harry Landis*
PRIVATE WILLIE MALTRAVERS	*Derek Nimmo*
SAM GOULANSKY	*Michael Segal*
LARRY HOFFMAN	*Hugh McDermott*
THE PRAWN	*Ernest Clark*
UNCLE JOE	*Reginald Gillam*

Directed by MURRAY MACDONALD

Décor by ANTHONY HOLLAND

The action of the Play passes in the living-room of Glenmally House, Argyll, the official residence of the General Officer Commanding, North-Western District

ACT I
A June morning

ACT II
An afternoon, three weeks later

ACT III
After dinner, the same evening

Time—the present

ACT I

SCENE—*The living-room of Glenmally House, Argyll, the official residence of the General Officer Commanding, North-Western District. A June morning.*

It is a large room with double doors up C leading to the entrance hall and other parts of the house. A door up R leads to the dining-room. French windows up L and LC lead on to a verandah and thence to the garden and river. There is a small window down L. The fireplace is R. Radiators stand against the wall R and L of the double doors. There is a large sofa RC with an occasional table L of it and a drum-table, on which there is a telephone, R of it. A third table is behind the sofa. An upright chair stands down R and there is a firestool in front of the fireplace. A small mahogany chest, with a marble top is in the corner up R. Between the french windows L, there is a large desk with chairs R and L of it. Another small mahogany chest is against the wall below the french windows LC, and a trolley with drinks is under the window down L. A refectory table is down L, with an armchair up R of it and an upright chair below it. An upholstered stool is R of the table. At night the room is lit by wall-brackets over the mantelpiece, a three-light desk lamp on the desk and table-lamps on the chest up R and on the chest down L. There are boxes of pink and white geraniums on the verandah. The hall is furnished with two chairs and an oak cupboard. The walls of the room are decorated with paintings, antlers and a regimental shield.

When the CURTAIN rises, sounds from the distant parade ground drift through the downstage french windows which are open. The upstage windows are closed. The double doors up C are open. CORPORAL SIDNEY GREEN is seated on the sofa, at the right end. He is in his early thirties and is senior N.C.O. of the General's domestic staff. He is wearing a green baize apron over his khaki shirt and trousers and is reading "The Sporting Life", and smoking a cigarette. PRIVATE BIDDY O'HARA, W.R.A.C., is dusting the desk. She is in her early twenties, and almost too shy to open her mouth. She wears her khaki uniform. After a moment, BIDDY goes out by the downstage french windows on to the verandah, shakes her duster then returns to her dusting.

CORPORAL (*from behind his newspaper*) Dodo O.K.?
BIDDY (*glancing out into the garden and nodding*) Yes, I think so. Her basket's only half full.
CORPORAL. Good. (*Having decided on the horse he wishes to back, he lowers his paper, reaches over to the telephone and lifts the receiver. Into the telephone*) Nobby? . . . Syd here . . . General still in his office? . . . Then listen . . . Put me five bob to win—"Grey Dancer" . . .

(BIDDY *turns to listen to the conversation*)

Landlord at *The Plough*. Got it straight from Lord Appleby's chauffeur . . . And five bob each way—"Take it Easy" . . . (*He crosses his legs upon the sofa and relaxes*) No, just a hunch . . .

(BIDDY *moves to the table* L *and dusts it*)

O.K.? . . . Tip me off when the old man leaves the camp. (*He replaces the receiver*)

BIDDY (*moving* LC) Why do you fancy "Take it Easy"?

CORPORAL (*smugly*) With the General going overseas today? It's too good to miss.

(PRIVATE SUZIE TIDMARSH, W.R.A.C., *enters from the hall. She is a flashy little minx, but on duty her blonde tresses are swept back in keeping with her khaki uniform. She is wearing her uniform at the moment and is carrying some unopened letters and some loose change. She goes to the table down* L. *The* CORPORAL *rises and folds the newspaper*)

SUZIE (*putting the letters on the table*) Hullo, Biddy.
BIDDY. Hullo, Suzie.
SUZIE (*crossing to the Corporal*) Hiya, Moonshine.
CORPORAL. Hiya, Livin' Doll.

(SUZIE, *giggling as she goes, crosses to the mantelpiece and puts the loose change on the downstage end of it*)

(*He watches Suzie with admiration*) What's that?

SUZIE (*turning*) Posty brought it. Some change for Dodo from the Naafi.

CORPORAL. Where's the account?

SUZIE. Wasn't one. General's wives don't worry about things like that.

(BIDDY *moves to the trolley* L *and dusts it*)

CORPORAL (*putting the newspaper in his apron pocket*) There's a sucker born every moment.

SUZIE (*waggling her hips*) You're telling me.

CORPORAL (*turning to Biddy*) Dodo still O.K.?

(SUZIE *takes this opportunity to steal a shilling from the loose change on the mantelpiece*)

BIDDY (*looking out of the french windows*) She's still at the sweet peas. I'd better do her bedroom.

(BIDDY *moves up* C *and exits to the hall, leaving the doors open.* SUZIE *crosses in front of the Corporal on her way out*)

CORPORAL (*intercepting Suzie*) Still want to see Loch Lomond?
SUZIE. You bet!
CORPORAL (*crossing to* R *of the table* R *of the sofa*) It's in the bag.

Photograph by Anthony Buckley

To face page 2 — The Amorous Prawn

(*He flicks his ash into the ashtray*) With the General overseas, all we'll have to do is spring clean the staff quarters.

Suzie. What about it?

Corporal (*moving to Suzie; confidently*) Take the afternoon off whenever we want it. The General's car is being de-coked.

Suzie (*impatiently*) Moonshine, what are you driving at?

Corporal (*chuckling*) Well, when it's got together again, it'll mean a trial run.

Suzie (*excitedly*) To Loch Lomond?

(*The* Corporal *is about to take Suzie in his arms when the telephone rings. He lifts the receiver*)

Corporal (*into the telephone; formally*) Glenmally House . . . (*With a sudden change of manner*) Thanks, chum. (*He slams down the receiver*) Quick, Suzie, the General's on his way. (*He stubs out his cigarette in the ashtray, crosses to the stool down* c, *picks up a silver tray containing two cigarette boxes, moves to the table down* l *and leaves the larger box on it, then crosses to the table* l *of the sofa and puts down the second box*)

(Suzie, *meanwhile, tidies the cushions on the sofa*)

Suzie (*leaning across the left arm of the sofa*) You really mean that, Moonshine?

Corporal. Mean what?

Suzie (*throwing her arms around his neck*) About Loch Lomond.

Corporal (*pushing her away*) Suzie, please. You heard what he said. Suppose the General was to walk in. I'd be in the glasshouse in no time. (*He moves below the sofa*)

(Suzie *tries to pinch a cigarette from the box on the table* l *of the sofa*)

(*He picks up the box and puts it on his tray*) That's enough of that. You've had more than your ration already.

(Suzie *replaces the cigarette in the box*)

Suzie (*waggling her bottom provocatively*) And that goes for you, too.

(Suzie *moves up* c *and exits to the hall, leaving the doors open. The* Corporal *takes a cigarette from the box, puts it behind his ear, then replaces the box on the table* l *of the sofa, leaving the lid open. He then crosses to the fireplace and puts his tray on the firestool.* Lady Fitzadam *enters by the downstage french windows. She is in her late forties and is extremely attractive. Socially she is a considerable asset to her husband's career, but the pomp and ceremony of military life bore her to distraction. She wears a smock-overall and is carrying a trug basket containing a bunch of sweet peas and a bunch of stock. She wears gardening gloves. She stands for a moment in the french windows watching the Corporal. The* Corporal, *unaware of Lady Fitzadam, takes a shilling from the loose change on the mantelpiece, and puts it in his pocket.*

LADY FITZADAM *moves to the table down* L *and puts her trug noisily on the upstage end of it. The* CORPORAL *jumps and busies himself pretending to read an invitation card which is propped on the mantelpiece*)

LADY FITZADAM. Bit jumpy this morning, aren't you, Corporal?

CORPORAL. Sorry, my lady. (*He picks up the invitation card and moves below the sofa*) I was just reading this invitation from Buckingham Palace . . .

LADY FITZADAM. The garden party?

CORPORAL. Yes, and sort of imagining myself among all those lords and ladies.

LADY FITZADAM. I'll try and bring you back a teaspoon with the royal coat of arms on it.

(*The sound of a car horn and the noise of sentries springing to attention is heard off* L)

CORPORAL. Excuse me, my lady. That'll be the General. (*He replaces the card on the mantelpiece, picks up his tray, and starts to go, removing his apron at the same time*)

LADY FITZADAM (*intercepting the Corporal*) Corporal.

CORPORAL. Yes, my lady?

LADY FITZADAM (*pointing to his ear*) I didn't know you had taken to filter tips.

(*The* CORPORAL *finds this too much for him and bolts out to the hall, leaving the doors open.* LADY FITZADAM *removes her gloves, drops them on the sofa, then crosses to the mantelpiece and examines the loose change. She then moves to the telephone and lifts the receiver*)

(*Into the telephone*) Exchange—get me the Naafi, please . . . Canteen manager. (*She replaces the receiver*)

(*The* CORPORAL *enters from the hall and stands to attention,* R *of the doorway.*

MAJOR-GENERAL SIR HAMISH FITZADAM, K.B.E., C.B., D.S.O., *enters from the hall. He is a fine upstanding figure in his late fifties. A rigid disciplinarian when on duty, he is kind and warm-hearted in the privacy of his home. He wears khaki uniform and carries a brief-case*)

GENERAL (*to the Corporal*) Have my bags down by eight minutes past—better make it seven—market day—might easily run into some sheep.

CORPORAL. Very good, sir.

(*The* CORPORAL *exits to the hall, closing the doors behind him. The* GENERAL *puts his brief-case on the desk, then crosses down* C. LADY FITZADAM *moves to* R *of the* GENERAL. *They embrace*)

GENERAL (*tenderly*) Well, my dear, almost zero hour.

LADY FITZADAM. Are you sure Huggins has packed everything?

GENERAL (*laughing*) Be the hell of a row if he hasn't.

LADY FITZADAM. Plenty of underclothes? It's bound to be hot crossing the Equator, and you know how damp underclothes . . .

GENERAL. Huggins hasn't been my batman for five years for nothing. (*He moves to the table down* L) Must you always throw your flowers down here, Dodo? Such bad luck on the staff after they've laid everything out so tidily. (*He picks up the letters, moves behind the desk, sits in the desk chair and opens the letters*)

(*The telephone rings.* LADY FITZADAM *moves to the telephone, lifts the receiver and sits on the sofa at the right end*)

LADY FITZADAM (*into the telephone*) Oh, is that you, Mr Wilson? . . . Lady Fitzadam here. That change you sent over, are you sure you haven't sent too much? . . . Oh, yes, I'd forgotten the dishcloths. How silly of me . . . Twelve and six . . . Seven and six change . . . Yes, that's quite right . . . So sorry.

GENERAL. What's the matter, Naafi doing you down?

LADY FITZADAM (*replacing the receiver*) Not the Naafi—they sent me seven and six change—now there is only five and six left. (*She puts the coins on the table* R *of the sofa, takes her shoes from under the table and during the following speeches changes from her gardening shoes*)

GENERAL. I suppose you're blaming the staff.

LADY FITZADAM. I never mentioned the staff.

GENERAL. But you implied it. You are always getting at them. That business last night with Private O'Hara . . .

LADY FITZADAM. If you prefer your salmon soaked in cream and your strawberries mashed in mayonnaise . . .

GENERAL. She was doing her best. We all make mistakes. The best staff we've ever had. You should see their Army papers, their conduct sheets. (*He rises, moves to the front of the desk, picks up his pipes and puts them into his brief-case, which he leaves on the downstage end of the desk*) Not one less than V.G. for character, and all hand-picked by my Personnel Officer.

(LADY FITZADAM *rises with her gardening shoes in one hand and picks up her gardening gloves from the sofa*)

LADY FITZADAM. Quite, quite, darling. They're a fine bunch. The finest staff in the world. (*She moves* C) Ready to lay down their lives for their General at his slightest word.

GENERAL. Certainly.

LADY FITZADAM. Disciplined, incorruptible . . .

GENERAL. Take Private Huggins—got a D.C.M. on D Day.

LADY FITZADAM. And ever since has got plastered on pay day. (*She moves above the left end of the sofa*)

GENERAL. You don't realize how lucky you are. Most house-wives would give their right hands to have as many servants as you have.

LADY FITZADAM. Possibly. But it so happens that I would prefer far fewer servants—or none at all—and be mistress of my own home. (*She throws the gardening shoes and gloves under the table above the sofa*)

GENERAL. But you are.

LADY FITZADAM (*picking up her handbag from the table above the sofa*) Of course I'm not. How can you expect a bunch of troops who've been brought up on the parade ground to have any respect for a mistress who doesn't even know how to form fours—or threes—or whatever they do? (*She moves* R *of the sofa*)

(*The* GENERAL *moves behind the desk, takes a box of a hundred cigarettes from the desk drawer, and puts it in his brief-case*)

GENERAL. Now, really . . .

LADY FITZADAM (*moving below the sofa*) And hadn't the gumption to engage them in the first place.

GENERAL. I'm sure that never enters their heads.

LADY FITZADAM (*sitting on the sofa at the left end*) And who doesn't even pay their wages. Can you blame them for only taking their orders from you, and treating me like a half-witted concubine?

GENERAL (*crossing to* L *of the sofa*) Dodo, you know that's not true.

LADY FITZADAM. But you wait, my boy, until the autumn when we've retired. We'll be lucky if we have one daily—probably over seventy and arthritic at that.

GENERAL (*kissing her head*) Seriously, darling. Will you miss it all very much?

LADY FITZADAM. What?

GENERAL. All this. This big house—grounds—fishing—five servants—gardeners galore—everyone at your beck and call.

LADY FITZADAM (*rising and crossing above the table down* L) Miss it? I can't wait to forget it.

GENERAL (*indicating the trug of flowers*) Dodo, just to make me very happy, could you put those flowers in a bowl somewhere? After all, the wretched staff . . . (*He sits in the armchair* LC)

LADY FITZADAM (*picking up the trug*) What heaven it will be. (*She crosses and puts the trug on the table behind the sofa*) Think of growing our own flowers that really belong to us.

(*The* GENERAL *picks up a letter from the desk and studies it*)

GENERAL. What on earth is this? Prawn Ffoulkes?

LADY FITZADAM. Who?

GENERAL (*reading from the envelope*) "Prawn Ffoulkes, Glenmally House."

LADY FITZADAM (*arranging the sweet peas in a vase on the table behind the sofa*) Didn't a Ffoulkes own this place before the war?

GENERAL. I believe you're right. But heaven knows where he lives now. (*He reads the letter*) "Dear Prawn—what do you know? I've just come across a programme for a *Bohemian Club* singsong back in thirty-two and on the back is written 'To Larry, the great guy in California. With admiration, The Prawn'." Oh, really, dear, we can't go on.

LADY FITZADAM (*crossing to the General*) Oh, yes, we must—(*she takes the letter from him*) I'm intrigued. (*She reads*) "So just in case this reaches you—Sam Goulansky—he's a sweet guy—and I, are sailing in the *Queen Mary*, arriving June the tenth."

GENERAL. But it's the twelfth now.

LADY FITZADAM (*reading*) "So, if ever you get time for a highball, we'll be at the *Savoy* in Strand Street."

GENERAL. "Strand Street"! Ha, ha, ha!

LADY FITZADAM. He sounds rather fun. I wonder who he is. (*She returns the letter to the General, moves to the table behind the sofa and continues with the flowers*)

GENERAL (*reading*) "A few days of doing the sights and then we're hoping for three or four weeks of that salmon fishing you used to talk about. Any ideas? In any case, all the best, Prawn, you wicked old lady-killer. Regards, Larry Hoffman." Better drop Mr Hoffman a line, telling him that for all we know the Prawn is dead.

LADY FITZADAM (*taking the vase of flowers and placing them on the radiator shelf up L*) In aspic, as you might say.

GENERAL. Very good, my dear. (*He laughs*)

LADY FITZADAM. Nothing from the house agent?

GENERAL. Yes, here it is. (*He puts the first letter on the desk, picks up a second letter and holds it out*)

(LADY FITZADAM *moves below the desk, takes the letter from the General and reads it*)

LADY FITZADAM. Ah! Oh, they won't take it.

GENERAL (*rising*) What?

LADY FITZADAM. Our offer. They say it's seven five or nothing.

GENERAL. That's too bad.

LADY FITZADAM (*reading*) "Seven thousand five hundred down for the house and garden or eight thousand to include the paddock."

GENERAL (*taking the letter from her*) Never mind, Dodo, darling. We'll be just as happy in Camberley.

LADY FITZADAM (*crossing below the General to the stool c*) But I don't want to live in Camberley. (*She picks up a magazine and points to a picture*) Beastly modern, suburban house. I want this house in Dorset.

GENERAL. But, Dodo, we've been into this so many times. I've discussed it with the bank manager until I'm blue in the face. (*He puts the agent's letter on the desk*) If we're going to have a car, all we can manage for the house is six and a half top.

(LADY FITZADAM *stares at a small modern type painting on the wall down R*)

And what's the good of having a house in the wilds of Dorset, if we can't even get to the station.

LADY FITZADAM. We could have a bicycle. If only I could sell some of my wretched paintings.

GENERAL (*turning and looking at the paintings*) Not on your life. I wouldn't part with one of them.

LADY FITZADAM (*crossing to the General and striking him on the back with the magazine*) That's all very well, but what we need is money.

GENERAL. Yes, I dare say, but . . .

LADY FITZADAM (*moving* C) There must be something we could sell.

GENERAL. Darling, you know we've tried everything.

LADY FITZADAM. This carpet, for instance.

GENERAL. That happens to belong to the Army.

LADY FITZADAM. I could replace it with a far cheaper one. (*She moves below the sofa*) No-one would ever know.

(*The* GENERAL *moves to Lady Fitzadam, takes the magazine from her and crosses to the fireplace*)

GENERAL (*shaking his head*) I'm afraid it's Camberley. Perhaps later on, if . . .

LADY FITZADAM (*pointing out of the french windows*) What about the new motor mower? That must be worth at least a couple of hundred.

GENERAL (*turning to her*) Unfortunately it has a large W.D. stamped on the side.

LADY FITZADAM. I know, let the salmon fishing. People pay the earth at this time of year.

GENERAL (*moving* R *of the sofa and throwing the magazine on it; patiently*) Dodo, I've done forty long and faithful years . . .

LADY FITZADAM (*moving to him*) That's what I mean. Forty years in which you've never taken the slightest advantage of any of the thousand and one perks held in front of your nose. You remember that smooth gentleman in Germany, who offered you a fortune for your surplus lorries?

GENERAL. He finished up in Wormwood Scrubbs. (*He turns away and presses the bell-push on the table* R *of the sofa*)

LADY FITZADAM. And yet, when an overworked General wants a paltry thousand pounds which is going to make all the difference to our old age . . .

GENERAL (*patting her shoulder and crossing to the desk*) I know, my dear. I'm sorry, but I must be on my way.

LADY FITZADAM (*moving to the fireplace*) Oh, dear!

(*The double doors are thrown open.*

The CORPORAL *enters up* C, *carrying the General's overcoat, which he puts over the back of the sofa.*

PRIVATE ALBERT HUGGINS *follows the Corporal on, carrying the General's cap, cane and gloves, which he puts on the upstage end of the desk.* HUGGINS *is an old sweat who is up to every trick to avoid the discomforts of military discipline*)

CORPORAL. All baggage loaded, sir. Car ready for departure.

(*The* GENERAL *picks up his brief-case and hands it to Huggins.*
LADY FITZADAM *removes her smock and puts it under the table behind the
sofa*)

GENERAL. Before I leave, Corporal Green, I would like to have
a few words with the staff.
CORPORAL (*anxiously*) Nothing wrong, I hope, sir?
GENERAL (*curtly*) Bring them in.
CORPORAL. Yes, sir.

(*The* CORPORAL *gives Huggins a nod to exit.*
HUGGINS *exits up* C.
The CORPORAL *follows Huggins off and closes the doors behind
him*)

GENERAL (*moving* C) Good-bye, darling. Look after yourself.
LADY FITZADAM (*moving to him*) Can't I come to the airport?
GENERAL. Sorry, I'm picking up the A.O.C. And you know the
regulations about wives travelling in official cars.
LADY FITZADAM. Blast the regulations!
GENERAL. Dodo!
LADY FITZADAM (*moving to the table behind the sofa*) I've brought
you a little present. (*She picks up a small parcel wrapped in tissue paper
and moves round the right end of the sofa*)
GENERAL (*moving to her*) Darling, how sweet of you. (*He takes the
parcel and unwraps it*)
LADY FITZADAM. I got them in Oban. All that high altitude
flying.
GENERAL (*displaying a pair of tartan ear-muffs*) What on earth . . . ?
LADY FITZADAM. Ear-muffs—like they wear for climbing moun-
tains. See if they fit.

(*The* GENERAL *dons the ear-muffs*)

I thought you'd like tartan ones to remind you of home.
GENERAL (*taking her in his arms and embracing her*) Darling, I can't
think of anything nicer. I'll wear them night and day.
CORPORAL (*off*) Quick march. Left, right, left, right . . .

(*The double doors burst open.*
SUZIE, BIDDY, PRIVATE WILLIE MALTRAVERS *and* HUGGINS
march on, followed by the CORPORAL. WILLIE *is a chef and slightly
precious. Bursting with culinary enthusiasm, he has only recently advanced
from the cookhouse to the General's residence. When* SUZIE *gets downstage
by the end of the table down* L, *the* CORPORAL *calls* "*Parade Halt, Right
Turn.*" *The others shuffle into line and take up their correct* "*dressing*".
LADY FITZADAM *moves to the fireplace, throws the tissue paper into it,
then sits on the firestool. The* CORPORAL *turns to address the General but
is startled to see him wearing the ear-muffs and stammers*)

All present and correct, sir.
GENERAL. Stand them at ease.
CORPORAL (*to the others*) Stand at ease!

(*The others stand at ease*)

GENERAL. Stand easy.

(*The others stand easy and react with amazement at seeing their General in ear-muffs*)

(*He is suddenly aware that he still wears the ear-muffs and in his embarrassment removes them and throws them on to the sofa*) No doubt you have been wondering while packing my tropical kit where I am off to. I expect the most popular bet has been East, Near, Middle or Far.
CORPORAL. That's right, sir.
GENERAL. Well, you're wrong. I'm going West. West to the Pacific to watch . . .
LADY FITZADAM. But surely you can go east to the Pacific?
GENERAL. Possibly, but I happen to be going west, via the United States. I'm going as military representative of Her Majesty's Government to witness some tests of high altitude missiles. I shall probably be away for at least two months—possibly three—depending on the weather, or should I say the two weathers . . .
LADY FITZADAM. Two what?
GENERAL. The weather in the sky, and whether the missiles go off.
CORPORAL (*laughing*) Oh, very good, sir. Ha, ha!

(*The others laugh except HUGGINS who gives a sudden belly laugh after everyone else has finished. The CORPORAL gives HUGGINS a black look which silences him*)

GENERAL. Normally my A.D.C. would have given you your orders in my absence—(*he moves down* C) but as Captain Montague may be quite a time recovering from his unfortunate polo accident, Lady Fitzadam will be in command while I am overseas——

(LADY FITZADAM *rises and moves to the table* R *of the sofa*)

—and I expect you to obey her orders just as you would mine. (*He moves to Lady Fitzadam*) While my wife may not be officially enrolled as a soldier of the Queen in the sense you and I are, I expect you to treat her—by virtue of her position—as your Commanding Officer. Is that clearly understood?

(*The others nod in agreement*)

And when I return, I shall expect to find the same standard of efficiency and cleanliness that has always been the recognized hallmark of this establishment. That's all, Corporal.
CORPORAL. Yes, sir. (*He takes a step forward*) And if I may say

so, sir—on behalf of all the staff, sir—we'd like to wish you *bon voyage*, sir.

WILLIE⎤
SUZIE ⎬ (*together*) Yes, sir.
BIDDY ⎦

(WILLIE *nudges Huggins*)

HUGGINS (*springing to attention*) Yes, sir.
GENERAL. Thank you. Thank you. (*He turns to Lady Fitzadam*)
CORPORAL (*turning and facing the others*) Parade shun.

(*The others spring to attention*)

Private Huggins, one pace forward, march.

(HUGGINS *steps one pace forward*)

Remainder right turn, quick march. Left, right, left, right.

(BIDDY, WILLIE *and* SUZIE *march off up* C, *leaving the doors open. The* CORPORAL *picks up the General's coat, while the* GENERAL *goes to the sofa and picks up the ear-muffs which he hands to Huggins.* HUGGINS *moves to the desk and picks up the General's hat, cane and gloves. The* GENERAL *is helped into his overcoat by the* CORPORAL, *who painstakingly removes a piece of fluff from the shoulder.* HUGGINS *then hands the* GENERAL *his cap, cane and gloves. The* GENERAL *puts on his cap and crosses to Lady Fitzadam, whilst putting on his gloves.* HUGGINS *shows the ear-muffs to the Corporal in bewilderment. The* CORPORAL *shrugs his shoulders. The* GENERAL *turns and glares at the Corporal with a look which clearly indicates that he wants to be left alone*)

(*Quickly*) Right turn, double march.

(*The* CORPORAL *and* HUGGINS *exit at the double up* C, *leaving the doors open. The* GENERAL *puts an arm around* LADY FITZADAM *and they stroll below the desk*)

GENERAL. Well, good-bye, darling. Look after yourself.
LADY FITZADAM. You're the one who's got to look after himself. All those thousands of miles across the Pacific.
GENERAL. I'll be all right. I can't wait for our retirement. And don't worry too much about Camberley. I could be happy with you anywhere.

(*They embrace, then the* GENERAL *moves to the doors up* C *and turns*)

LADY FITZADAM. Good-bye, Hamish.
GENERAL. I'll ring you from the airport.

(*The* GENERAL *salutes and exits up* C. LADY FITZADAM *wanders to the double doors and closes them. The sound is heard of troops being brought to attention and a car driving away.* LADY FITZADAM *moves to the sofa, picks up her jacket and puts it on, then crosses to the desk, picks up Prawn's letter and reads from it*)

LADY FITZADAM (*reading*) "... three or four weeks of that salmon fishing you used to talk about—any ideas?" (*She crosses to the telephone and lifts the receiver. Into the telephone*) Oh, exchange—get me telegrams, please. (*She puts the receiver on the table, then sits on the sofa at the right end and looks at the letter*) "Any ideas . . ." (*She picks up the receiver. Into the telephone*) Exchange—on second thoughts, don't worry about telegrams for the moment, I'd like to speak to the local house agent first. The one in Oban . . . That's right—McLeod. (*She waits to be connected*) Oh, hello, Mr McLeod . . . Lady Fitzadam here . . . I've had an enquiry from friends in America wanting to come to these parts to fish—and I—I mean they want to know how much it will cost . . . Something like the stretch going through our grounds . . . Would you really, now? . . . As much as that? . . . So two rods for four weeks will cost? . . . Two hundred pounds! . . . Fancy. And how about accommodation? You know how fastidious Americans are— central heating, lots of good food and first-class service . . . Yes, Mr McLeod, I know that very few houses in these parts have central heating and that good cooks and servants are practically unobtainable—but just supposing a comfortable house could be found with central heating—five servants—(*she presses the bell-push*) good fishing . . . But I do believe in fairies . . . You'd ask seven fifty? . . . Thank you, Mr McLeod—thank you very much. (*She replaces the receiver*)

(*The* CORPORAL *enters up* c)

CORPORAL (*moving to* L *of the sofa*) You rang, my lady?
LADY FITZADAM. Yes, Corporal. I'd like a few words with the staff.
CORPORAL (*anxiously*) Nothing wrong, my lady?
LADY FITZADAM. An order should never be questioned, Corporal, until after it has been carried out. (*She rises, picks up the magazine and puts it on the fire-stool*)
CORPORAL. Very good, my lady.

(*The* CORPORAL *exits up* c. LADY FITZADAM *turns to the telephone and lifts the receiver*)

LADY FITZADAM (*into the telephone*) Oh, exchange, don't worry about telegrams, get me a trunk call to London instead . . . Yes, on the General's private account . . . A personal call to—(*she looks at the letter*) a Mr Larry Hoffman at the *Savoy Hotel* . . . That's right— Hoffman. (*She replaces the receiver and picks up the loose change*)
CORPORAL (*off*) Left, right, left, right, left right.

(*The double doors burst open.*
SUZIE, BIDDY, WILLIE, HUGGINS *and the* CORPORAL *march on up* c. LADY FITZADAM *moves to the fireplace and puts the letter in her bag*)

Parade halt. Right turn. Stand at ease.
LADY FITZADAM. Stand easy.

(*The others stand easy*)

(*She moves below the sofa*) Now, you all heard what the General said about obeying orders whilst he's overseas. Well, I've decided that it's time there were one or two changes in this establishment. (*She moves to* L *of the sofa*) Some of us have got into some rather bad habits. We're far too inclined to take things—for granted. So I'm considering a re-shuffle—a change of tactics—in fact a brand new operation.

(*The others stare at her in amazement*)

(*She moves to the fireplace*) And to give it the sort of code name, to which your military training has accustomed you, I think we might call it—"Operation Lolly". (*She puts the loose change on the mantelpiece*)

CORPORAL (*taking two steps forward*) If you're talking about the Naafi change . . . ?

SUZIE (*moving to* L *of the Corporal*) Don't think you can blame it on me, Moonshine.

CORPORAL. Fall in! Fall in!

LADY FITZADAM. Please! Please!

(SUZIE *goes back into line*)

As far as I know, I never mentioned any Naafi change. All the same, thank you for the information.

(*The* CORPORAL *and* SUZIE *exchange black looks*)

(*She moves* C) With the General away—no official guests or parties, and only myself to look after—I've a feeling time may hang heavily on your hands.

CORPORAL (*quickly*) We were going to spring clean the staff quarters.

LADY FITZADAM. That should take three days at the outside, and the General is away for at least two months. (*She moves* RC) I propose to take in lodgers.

CORPORAL (*with an outraged look at the others*) Lodgers!

LADY FITZADAM. Or shall we say—paying guests?

CORPORAL (*smugly*) Of course, it's your affair, my lady, not mine, but I should have thought this being a military establishment maintained by the War Office, and paid for by the tax-payer— (*he indicates the others*) and we being military personnel serving Her Majesty, it would seem . . . (*He pauses*)

LADY FITZADAM (*icily*) Yes, Corporal.

CORPORAL. It would seem—as you might say—that some people —my Member of Parliament, for instance—might ask awkward questions if Headquarters North-Western District were being used for strawberry teas for trippers.

LADY FITZADAM. I've no intention of serving strawberry teas to trippers, but I see your point. (*She moves down* C *and circles to the fire-*

B

place) Under the circumstances, then I have no alternative but to return all surplus staff to full parade-ground duties.

(*This bombshell has an immediate effect on the others*)

HUGGINS (*stepping forward*) Permission to speak?

LADY FITZADAM. Granted.

HUGGINS. The doctor down the depot excused me all marching, 'ammer toes—sledge-'ammer toes, he called 'em.

LADY FITZADAM. You can explain that to the sergeant-major, Huggins. All right, Corporal. You may dismiss. (*She moves to lift the telephone receiver*)

(*The* CORPORAL *dashes forward and intercepts Lady Fitzadam*)

CORPORAL. Just a minute, my lady, you don't want to act too hasty. Perhaps if there weren't too many visitors . . .

LADY FITZADAM. At present I'm thinking in terms of two.

CORPORAL (*moving below the sofa*) Two? Ah, well, that's a different matter altogether.

LADY FITZADAM. You don't think your M.P. would object to two?

(*The* CORPORAL *realizes he is losing face all round*)

CORPORAL. As senior N.C.O., my lady, might I have a word—in private—with the other members of the staff?

LADY FITZADAM. Certainly. I'll be in the garden. (*She picks up her belt from the sofa, crosses below the Corporal and pauses in front of Huggins*) Excuse me.

(HUGGINS *steps aside.*

LADY FITZADAM *passes through the line and exits by the downstage french windows. After she has gone the* CORPORAL *goes to the double doors and closes them*)

HUGGINS (*crossing to the fireplace*) Put your bleedin' foot right in it, didn't yer? Nice cushy job, 'ere, and now . . .

CORPORAL (*moving down* C) All right, all right.

HUGGINS. If you'd been in the Army as long as wot I had, you'd know when you were well orf.

CORPORAL (*moving to* L *of the sofa*) If I'd been in the Army as long as you have, I'd be a field-marshal, writing my memoirs. (*He sits on the sofa at the left end*)

SUZIE (*moving to* L *of the sofa*) Belt up, you two. As I see it, it's this way. If we stay here, we'll be doing no more work than we did in the past. But if we have to go back to barracks . . . You should have heard what one of the girls in the canteen said—on her knees scrubbing all day long.

(BIDDY *sits in the chair down* L)

WILLIE (*moving up* L *of Suzie; deeply pained*) As for the cookhouse —murder.

CORPORAL. So you're in favour of stopping here?

SUZIE. You bet.

CORPORAL (*to Huggins*) And you?

HUGGINS. Don't ask stupid questions.

CORPORAL (*rising*) What about you, Willie?

WILLIE. As I told you, I once did three months in the cookhouse —roast beef—Irish stew—roast beef—Irish stew—purgatory.

(*The* CORPORAL *crosses to Biddy. While his back is turned,* HUGGINS *steals a shilling from the loose change on the mantelpiece, then sits on the firestool*)

CORPORAL. What about you, Biddy?

(BIDDY *is too shy to speak but nods vigorously*)

So I take it we're all in favour?

(BIDDY *holds up her hand and the rest nod agreement*)

And, of course, if Dodo tries to work a quick one—work us in the afternoon or anything like that—(*he crosses to Huggins*) we've always got my M.P. up our sleeve.

HUGGINS (*contemptuously*) You can keep 'im up your sleeve. Stuff him right up your bleeding armpit.

(*The* CORPORAL *crosses to* C *as though going to call Lady Fitzadam, then stops*)

CORPORAL. All right, then, get fell in.

(*The others get into line*)

(*He crosses to the french windows and calls*) All right now, my lady. (*He moves and stands at the head of the line*)

(LADY FITZADAM *enters by the french windows and stops behind Huggins*)

LADY FITZADAM. Excuse me.

(HUGGINS *steps aside*)

(*She passes through the line, crosses below the sofa, then stops and turns*) Secret ballot over?

CORPORAL (*stepping forward; smugly*) We have decided, that rather than desert our posts in the General's absence . . .

LADY FITZADAM. I'm sure he'll be deeply touched. Besides, think of the extra lolly you'd be deserting.

CORPORAL (*taken aback*) Lolly?

LADY FITZADAM (*moving to the fireplace*) Lots and lots of lovely lolly. (*She notices another shilling is missing*) Couldn't you relax them a little?

CORPORAL (*looking at the others*) They're at ease now.

LADY FITZADAM. They don't look it. Biddy, try this sofa. It's quite comfortable.

(BIDDY *hesitates.* WILLIE *pushes her slightly and* BIDDY *sits on the sofa at the right end*)

Take that chair, Suzie.

(SUZIE *sits on the chair down* L)

Maltravers—it's Willie, isn't it? Beside Biddy.

(WILLIE *crosses gingerly and sits* L *of Biddy on the sofa.* HUGGINS *carefully places himself in front of the armchair* LC)

Huggins.

HUGGINS (*springing to attention*) Sir!

CORPORAL. Sit!

(HUGGINS *sits in the armchair* LC, *looking most uncomfortable*)

LADY FITZADAM (*indicating the chair* R *of the desk*) Draw up that chair, Corporal.

(*The* CORPORAL *draws the chair forward and sits in it*)

(*She sits on the sofa at the left end*) Now, isn't this nice and cosy?

(*Everyone is looking far from cosy or comfortable*)

What about a drink? Suzie, you know where they are?

SUZIE (*rising*) Yes, my lady. (*She crosses to the trolley* L)

LADY FITZADAM. Huggins, what will you have.

HUGGINS. I'll have a Scotch, my lady.

LADY FITZADAM. Corporal?

CORPORAL. Whisky, please. (*He removes his cap and puts it under his shoulder strap*)

LADY FITZADAM. Biddy?

BIDDY. Bitter lemon.

WILLIE. Gin and tonic.

LADY FITZADAM. And I'll have a gin and tonic. Give Suzie a hand, will you, Corporal.

(*The* CORPORAL *rises, crosses to the trolley and assists* SUZIE *to prepare the drinks*)

Of course, our guests must obviously have no idea that we are a military establishment. Not only might it lead to awkward complications, but it could also have a disastrous effect on their generosity. So often have I been shocked by the meanness of our official guests.

(*The* CORPORAL *brings a tray with drinks for* LADY FITZADAM, BIDDY *and* WILLIE)

The number of times I've noticed a miserable half crown lying on the dressing-room table.

CORPORAL. Lucky if it's that.
LADY FITZADAM (*passing the drinks*) Biddy—Willie. (*She takes her own drink*) Thank you. On the other hand, waiters and chambermaids in London earn quite fabulous sums in tips.
CORPORAL (*returning to the trolley*) You're telling us.
LADY FITZADAM. I hope the same will happen here.

(*The* CORPORAL *picks up two whiskies, hands one to* HUGGINS *and keeps one for himself.* SUZIE *takes her drink and sits in the chair down* L)

CORPORAL. How do you think we should organize this, my lady? Pool and share out, or every man for himself?
LADY FITZADAM. Not so fast, Corporal. That's a detail we can discuss later. First the main principles. (*She raises her glass*) Cheers.

(*They all sip their drinks except* HUGGINS *who gulps his back and puts the glass noisily on the table down* L. *The remainder of the staff glare at this breach of good manners*)

Suzie, pass round the cigarette box, will you?

(SUZIE *passes the box from the table down* L *to Huggins.* LADY FITZADAM *takes the box from the table* L *of the sofa and offers it to* WILLIE, *who takes a cigarette. She is about to take a cigarette for herself when the* CORPORAL *takes a packet of twenty Players from his pocket*)

CORPORAL (*offering the packet to Lady Fitzadam*) Here, have one of mine.
LADY FITZADAM (*pointedly*) Given up filter tips, Corporal? (*She takes a cigarette from the Corporal's packet*)

(HUGGINS *delights in the* CORPORAL's *discomfort.* WILLIE *lights Lady Fitzadam's cigarette and his own. The* CORPORAL *lights a cigarette from his packet with the table lighter on the table* L *of the sofa*)

(*She rises and moves to the fireplace*) Top secrecy—and in particular the keeping of the truth away from our guests—is obviously essential. To ensure this, I suggest we form ourselves into a limited company with the staff taking a share of the profits. All agreed?

(*There is a general show of hands*)

From the day our first guests arrive, uniform will, of course, become a thing of the past. (*She crosses to* R *of the Corporal*) You, Corporal, will dress as *maitre d'hôtel*.
CORPORAL. Come again?
LADY FITZADAM. Sort of general manager. (*She turns to Willie*) You, Willie, as chef, will have a position of tremendous responsibility. Our cuisine must become a byword.
WILLIE (*excitedly*) Provided I'm allowed the necessary ingredients.
LADY FITZADAM (*crossing to the fireplace*) I know what you mean. The General's somewhat conservative tastes—his mania for grilled

kippers and scrambled eggs—have proved a little monotonous. In the future . . .

(WILLIE *leaps to his feet and advances on* LADY FITZADAM *who retreats down* R)

WILLIE. Madam, my mind is reeling with menus. Some ice cold Vichysoise—Sole Veronique cooked in white sauce with grapes and a sauce de Wilhelm, my own specialite . . .

LADY FITZADAM (*interrupting the flow*) That sounds delicious, Willie. (*She crosses and stands in front of the sofa*)

CORPORAL. What about the sentries?

LADY FITZADAM. What about them?

(WILLIE *resumes his seat on the sofa*)

CORPORAL. Suppose they do a "Halt, who goes there?"

LADY FITZADAM. Why on earth should they? (*She moves to* R *of the Corporal*) On principle, they always present arms to everyone from the baker's boy upwards.

CORPORAL. I was thinking of "our guests". Won't they think it strange having bayonets waving all over the shop?

LADY FITZADAM. A very good point. (*She crosses to the desk and picks up a pad and pencil*) I'll ask their Company Commander if they can be given other duties during the General's absence.

CORPORAL. Good idea.

HUGGINS (*rising*) Permission to speak.

CORPORAL. Stop being so Army.

HUGGINS (*to the others*) The Company Commander might send them So-and-so's back to the parade ground. Bit of square bashin' and a few extra fatigues . . .

(*The* CORPORAL *glares at* HUGGINS *who breaks off*)

LADY FITZADAM (*turning from the desk*) Huggins!

HUGGINS (*springing to attention*) Sir!

LADY FITZADAM (*crossing to* RC) Huggins, you must try and control yourself. A false move like that could wreck the whole show.

CORPORAL. Relax, chum. You're in civvy street, now.

(HUGGINS *flicks his cigarette ash on to the carpet and subsides into his chair*)

LADY FITZADAM. As an experienced batman, you should find no difficulties in carrying out the duties of valet.

CORPORAL. Only don't put out no spurs with their evening dress.

LADY FITZADAM. And you, Biddy, will be chambermaid upstairs, while Suzie as parlourmaid remains downstairs.

CORPORAL. That's right. Must keep the place respectable.

LADY FITZADAM (*moving to the fireplace and turning*) When not driving the car, Mac will, of course, act as ghillie on the river. Let's pray the fish are running.

CORPORAL. How about Uncle Joe?

LADY FITZADAM. Who?

CORPORAL. Mac's uncle. The landlord at the local says he's one of the best poachers in the world.

LADY FITZADAM. What about it?

CORPORAL. Well, if they don't strike it lucky on our bit of river, Uncle Joe might know of another stretch where they could get one on the sly.

LADY FITZADAM (*delighted*) Good idea.

CORPORAL. It just came to me.

LADY FITZADAM. Now, about myself. Obviously I mustn't be referred to as the General's wife.

WILLIE. No, no. That would never do.

LADY FITZADAM. So perhaps I'd better become a widow.

BIDDY (*horrified*) Kill the General?

LADY FITZADAM. Only figuratively, Biddy. Only to mislead our visitors. (*She moves below the left end of the sofa*) I wonder what my husband was? Any ideas?

CORPORAL. Bookmaker?

LADY FITZADAM. That might lead to awkward questions about horses. Besides, a bookmaker's widow would never have to take in paying guests. (*She sits on the sofa at the left end*)

SUZIE. What about a dance-band leader, my lady?

LADY FITZADAM. No. One of them might happen to be a musician. They'd rumble that in no time.

WILLIE. Hotelier any good?

LADY FITZADAM. They'd ask where. I'd be in trouble right away. No. (*She rises and crosses to R of the Corporal*) It's got to be something the average person knows nothing about.

HUGGINS (*springing to attention*) Permission to speak.

LADY FITZADAM (*startled*) Don't do that, Huggins. Granted.

HUGGINS. How about a doctor wot's got put inside for insanitary operations?

(LADY FITZADAM *smothers her laughter and moves below the left end of the sofa*)

CORPORAL (*rising*) Turn it up. Sorry, my lady. (*He crosses above his chair and puts his glass on the trolley. Apologetically*) Huggins did two years with the Marines.

(BIDDY *rises, crosses to Lady Fitzadam and whispers to her.* HUGGINS *resumes his seat.* WILLIE *moves into Biddy's seat on the sofa*)

LADY FITZADAM. What a good idea, Biddy—a scientist. (*She turns to the others*) Beautifully vague—every chance of being evasive. Don't you agree?

(*The others nod except* WILLIE *who looks adoringly at* BIDDY *and pulls her down to sit* L *of himself on the sofa*)

Willie. A scientist! Brilliant, Biddykins.

Lady Fitzadam (*moving to the chair* c *and sitting*) Poor Archie—I think Archie's a good name, don't you?

Corporal (*moving slightly towards her*) Come again?

Lady Fitzadam. For my husband, the scientist?

Corporal (*crossing to* l *of Lady Fitzadam*) Archibald sounds more scientific.

Lady Fitzadam. Poor Archibald. Such a brilliant man. He was working on something terribly hush-hush—so secret, he couldn't even tell me. Then one day—just after they'd taken him a cup of tea—poof! And he'd gone.

Corporal (*crossing to* l *of the sofa*) What a line shoot. Fancy you thinking of that. I like that little touch about the tea. (*He sits on the sofa at the left end*) Real artistic.

Lady Fitzadam. Well, now we're all in this—how shall I put it —in this little fiddle together, never let us forget the old axiom "Honour amongst thieves".

Corporal (*boisterously*) That's good. That's real good. I like that.

Lady Fitzadam (*pointedly*) I thought you would. (*She holds out her hand*) That small matter of the Naafi change, for instance?

(Huggins *looks sheepish. The* Corporal *rises, takes a shilling from his pocket and hands it to Lady Fitzadam. He then moves and stands above the left end of the sofa*)

Suzie?

(Suzie *rises, hands Lady Fitzadam a shilling, then resumes her seat*)

Any others? (*She holds out her hand to Huggins*)

(Huggins *rises reluctantly, takes a shilling from his pocket and hands it to Lady Fitzadam*)

Well now, I think we all understand each other?

Corporal. Yes, madam.

(*The telephone rings*)

Lady Fitzadam (*rising*) That must be the General. That'll be all for now.

Corporal. Fall in!

(Lady Fitzadam *crosses to the telephone. The others jump into line. The* Corporal *replaces the chair* r *of the desk.* Lady Fitzadam *lifts the receiver and puts her hand over it*)

Lady Fitzadam. Make all the General's favourite noises. It will send him off in such a happy mood. (*She uncovers the receiver*)

Corporal (*standing above the sofa; loudly*) Parade shun! Right wheel, quick march. Left, right, left right, left, right. (*He opens the double doors*)

(LADY FITZADAM *holds the receiver down to pick up the sound of their marching feet. The staff march around in front of the sofa, stamping as they pass the receiver. They circle round and exit up* C.

The CORPORAL *follows the others off, still giving orders and making the "thumbs up" sign as he closes the doors*)

LADY FITZADAM (*into the telephone*) Hullo, darling . . . (*Her expression changes*) Oh, it's you, Mr Hoffman . . . What's that? . . . (*She sits on the sofa at the right end*) No, no-one's being murdered—just some of my guests getting worked up about who caught the most salmon . . . I'm afraid your friend Mr Ffoulkes left here years ago . . . No, no, I run it as a guest-house . . . Central heating? . . . Dear me, yes, in every room . . . Liquor? We have the reputation—if I may say so —of having the finest cellars north of the Tweed . . . Big what? . . . Oh, you mean those sort of steaks . . . For a moment I thought you were talking about roulette . . . Nothing but the best local Aberdeen Angus or prime Hereford, according to your taste . . . (*She rises and picks up the magazine from the firestool*) Just let me look at the bookings. (*She looks at the picture of Gundog Manor*) Two singles for five weeks? . . . Yes, I think we could manage that . . .

The CURTAIN *quickly falls*

ACT II

SCENE—*The same. A fortnight later. Afternoon.*
The desk chair has been removed, the desk reversed and placed against the wall L, *with the chair up* LC *now set to the desk. A trolley with tea for one is set above the stool* L.

When the CURTAIN *rises,* SAM GOULANSKY *is seated on the sofa, at the right end, with* SUZIE *in his arms.* SAM *is a middle-aged, slightly plump American, wearing spectacles. Beneath a brash Brooklyn exterior, there beats a heart of gold. He wears an American type sports jacket and grey flannels. It is a very changed* SUZIE. *She now wears a tight skirt and jersey and her blonde tresses fall down to her shoulders. After a few moments,* SUZIE *frees herself.*

SAM. Hey, come back. (*He grabs Suzie and smothers her again*)

(*The* CORPORAL, *unseen by the others, enters up* C. *He wears smart morning clothes and carries an account book, two pay sheets and a clipboard, four pay packets, filled and sealed and a bundle of pound notes. He sees what is going on, glares angrily and is about to go.*
LADY FITZADAM *enters by the upstage french windows. She carries her handbag. She whispers to the Corporal.*
The CORPORAL *exits up* C, *leaving the door open*)

LADY FITZADAM (*after a pause; calling*) Oh, Mr Green.

(SAM *and* SUZIE *part hastily*)

CORPORAL (*off*) Yes, madam?

(SUZIE, *in her rush to get up, knocks* SAM *on to the floor. He picks himself up and searches for his glasses which he finds and puts on.* SUZIE *goes to the fireplace and stands in front of it*)

LADY FITZADAM. Why, if it isn't Mr Goulansky.

(*The* CORPORAL *enters up* C *and closes the doors*)

(*She moves to the tea trolley*) Suzie been giving you some tea?
SAM. That's right, ma'am.
LADY FITZADAM (*examining the trolley*) Everything to your satisfaction?
SAM (*looking at Suzie*) I'll say!

(*The* CORPORAL *moves to the table down* L)

LADY FITZADAM. We do our best to please. (*She lifts the cover of the hotplate*) Ah! "Gentleman's Relish." Such a fascinating name, I always think.

SAM. You're telling me.

LADY FITZADAM (*moving to* L *of the sofa*) Mr Hoffman has just landed a twenty-two pounder.

SAM. Larry did that?

LADY FITZADAM. Mac says he's never seen a finer fish outside Lord Appleby's water.

SAM (*crossing below Lady Fitzadam to face the Corporal*) But Larry told me Mac was driving him over to look at some ruined castle.

LADY FITZADAM. Far from it. He's so excited, he's trying for another while his eye's in.

SAM. The big heel! I'll get even with him, if it's the last thing I do.

(SAM *rushes out by the downstage french windows, passes along the verandah and exits up* L)

LADY FITZADAM. Nice work, Suzie. The sort of gallant service that wins quick promotion.

CORPORAL (*moving* LC) Careful, Private Tidmarsh, or you'll find yourself a four-star General.

LADY FITZADAM (*crossing above the sofa to* R *of it*) Or better still, we'll be a four-star hotel.

(SUZIE *minces across to the Corporal, holding out a brooch*)

CORPORAL. What's that?

SUZIE. Sparklers. (*She turns to Lady Fitzadam*) Do I have to put this in the pool?

CORPORAL. Of course.

LADY FITZADAM (*moving to Suzie and pinning the brooch on her*) Perhaps, Corporal, we should look on this as a personal decoration for loyal self-sacrifice.

CORPORAL. Self-sacrifice? Her?

LADY FITZADAM (*moving below the right end of the sofa; to Suzie*) Remind me to write you out a citation.

SUZIE. Oh, thank you, madam. Bad luck, Moonshine. (*She runs her fingers up his arm*)

CORPORAL (*pushing Suzie away*) That's quite enough of that. (*He indicates the tea trolley*) Clear those things away. (*He moves to the doors up* C *and opens them*)

(SUZIE *crosses to the tea trolley, wheels it up* C, *then stops and turns*)

SUZIE (*to Lady Fitzadam*) Remember that "how-d'you-do" over the Naafi change?

LADY FITZADAM. Indeed I do.

SUZIE (*looking at the Corporal*) Just amateurs, weren't we?

(SUZIE *laughs and exits up* C *with the trolley. The* CORPORAL *closes the doors.* LADY FITZADAM *goes to the fireplace, removes the firescreen and moves it down* R)

LADY FITZADAM. Suzie certainly seems to be entering into the spirit of things.

CORPORAL (*moving down* c) I'd have you know, madam, that before this guest-house skylark, Suzie and me was walking out. Doing all right, I was, but now, with all these sparklers . . .

LADY FITZADAM. Don't worry, Mr Green—our guests are only here for another ten days.

CORPORAL. At his speed, he'll only need ten minutes.

(LADY FITZADAM *takes a cashbox from its hiding-place in the fire-grate and puts it on the firestool*)

LADY FITZADAM. Suzie knows how to look after herself.

CORPORAL. You're telling me!

LADY FITZADAM. And never forget the regimental motto. (*She points to the shield on the wall down* R) "*Servus super ego.*"

CORPORAL (*moving to* L *of the sofa*) Come again?

LADY FITZADAM. "Service above self." Or in other words—"the customer is always right".

CORPORAL (*moving to* L *of Lady Fitzadam*) That's all very well, my lady . . .

LADY FITZADAM (*sharply*) Mr Green!

CORPORAL. Sorry. I meant—madam. (*He crosses to* L *of the table down* L)

LADY FITZADAM (*crossing to the table down* L) Now for the week's report. (*She sits in the armchair* LC) How much in the kitty?

(*The* CORPORAL *puts down his clipboard, pay packets and account book, and counts his bundle of notes*)

(*She points to the pay packets*) What are these?

CORPORAL. I drew it up at the camp. Their army pay—chicken feed. (*He puts thirty-five pounds in notes on the table*) This is the stuff that matters.

LADY FITZADAM (*taking a notebook and pencil from her bag*) How much?

CORPORAL. Thirty-five quid.

LADY FITZADAM. All in tips? (*She notes the amount in her notebook*)

CORPORAL. Two quid they gave to Biddy for bringing them breakfast in bed.

LADY FITZADAM. Just as well Biddy's upstairs and Suzie's on the ground floor.

CORPORAL. You're telling me!

LADY FITZADAM (*pointing to the notes*) And the rest?

CORPORAL. A quid to Willie for doing their steaks a treat.

LADY FITZADAM. Yes?

CORPORAL (*crossing above Lady Fitzadam to* R *of her*) A quid to me from Mr Goulansky—here's poetic injustic for you—for arranging for Suzie to meet him in the greenhouse.

LADY FITZADAM. The customer is always right. (*She hands him a pound note*) But perhaps, like Suzie's brooch, we could look on this as an act of personal devotion. Next?

CORPORAL. Three quid Huggins.

LADY FITZADAM (*surprised*) What on earth for?

CORPORAL. Reciting "Gunga Din". Fair slays 'em, so he does. You ought to see him in the General's coat and cap. Looks real War Office.

LADY FITZADAM. I can't wait! And what did Mac get?

CORPORAL. All the rest.

LADY FITZADAM (*holding up the notes*) All this?

CORPORAL. Aye. Probably even more next week. They're getting that worked up about who catches the most, they've gone up to a fiver a fish.

LADY FITZADAM. Has either of our guests actually hooked one?

CORPORAL. Not on your life. But each time one of them gets left by himself, Mac slips a fish out of the bushes, and Bob's your uncle.

LADY FITZADAM. And whichever it is bribes Mac not to say a word to the other?

CORPORAL. That's the ticket!

LADY FITZADAM (*approvingly*) A very equitable arrangement. How much are we paying Mac's Uncle Joe?

CORPORAL. For poaching? Quid a fish, and if you ask me, that's cheap at the price. Night after night, the old geyser's up to his armpits in cold water. It's doing his rheumatics no good at all.

LADY FITZADAM. Tell Mac from me that in future Uncle Joe will get thirty bob a fish.

CORPORAL. Thirty bob! He'll dive in and spear them for that.

(LADY FITZADAM *rises, puts her notebook and pencil in her handbag, picks up the notes and crosses to the fireplace*)

LADY FITZADAM. Right! This week we'll have a share out of a fiver a head, and I'll bank the rest for a rainy day. Anything else to report?

CORPORAL (*moving down* C) Don't think so. Willie's got his usual bleat.

LADY FITZADAM. I'd better see him.

(*The* CORPORAL *exits up* C. LADY FITZADAM *puts four pounds of the notes in the cashbox, then picks up an unopened telegram from the mantelpiece and looks at it, wondering about its contents.*

The CORPORAL *re-enters up* C, *closing the door behind him*)

CORPORAL. Won't be long. Just mashing the spuds.

LADY FITZADAM (*moving below the sofa*) I hope this cable for Mr Hoffman isn't bad news. Put it on the desk, will you?

(*The* CORPORAL *takes the telegram and puts it on the desk*)

(*She returns to the fireplace*) Tragic if they had to leave just as things are going so well.

CORPORAL (*mysteriously*) Better than you think.
LADY FITZADAM. How do you mean?
CORPORAL (*pointing to the picture over the desk*) Lucky you didn't sign these.
LADY FITZADAM. What is all this?
CORPORAL. Got the idea from Mac. Playing one fish against the other.
LADY FITZADAM (*moving below the right end of the sofa*) What on earth have fish got to do with my paintings?
CORPORAL (*crossing to L of Lady Fitzadam; confidentially*) I'm getting that Goulansky bloke all steamed up about them. Told him they were left to you by your auntie, and you know nothing about them. See what I mean?
LADY FITZADAM. I'm afraid I don't.
CORPORAL. I mean—what they're really worth. And an art dealer had offered me a rake-off if I could get 'em for him cheap.
LADY FITZADAM. But they're worth absolutely nothing.
CORPORAL. Maybe. But Goulansky thinks the art dealer offered fifty.
LADY FITZADAM (*stunned*) Fifty pounds a painting?
CORPORAL. So if I get Hoffman interested, and work as one against the other like the fish . . .
LADY FITZADAM (*horrified*) But you can't do this. It's taking money under false pretences.
CORPORAL (*indignantly*) After what he's been doing to my Suzie?
LADY FITZADAM (*weakening*) You mean—all's fair in love and war?
CORPORAL (*moving slightly L*) Exactly. If they care to believe they're Zardeens, that's their look out.
LADY FITZADAM. Zardeens?
CORPORAL. The famous Zardeen. I made it up. Not bad, eh? On a par with your Archibald and his cup of tea.

(WILLIE *enters up* C. *He wears a chef's white overall and cap.* LADY FITZADAM *crosses to the fireplace. The* CORPORAL *crosses to the table down* L)

WILLIE. Yes?
CORPORAL. Army pay. Sign here.

(WILLIE *closes the door, moves to the table down* L, *signs and collects his pay packet from the* CORPORAL. *He then turns and moves towards the doors up* C)

LADY FITZADAM. Lolly!

(WILLIE *crosses to* LADY FITZADAM *who hands him five pounds*)

WILLIE. Thank you, madam. (*He moves to the doors up* C)
LADY FITZADAM. What's the matter, Willie?

(WILLIE *stops and turns*)

WILLIE. I'm not one to give trouble, and I'm not easily upset. but I can't stand the monotony another minute. I'm giving notice.

CORPORAL (*moving up* LC) Deserting?

WILLIE (*to the Corporal*) Do you mind? (*To Lady Fitzadam*) I want to go back to the cookhouse. Goodness knows, there was little enough variety there, but these Americans—one more order of "one rare— one medium rare" . . . Don't they eat anything else but steaks?

LADY FITZADAM. Don't worry, Willie—I've got some other guests coming.

CORPORAL. Oh. Who?

LADY FITZADAM. A Mr and Mrs Vernon from Oban, and by the tone of his voice he sounded very much the gourmet and just your cup of tea.

WILLIE (*crossing to* L *of Lady Fitzadam*) All I need is a little encouragement. I like to suggest new dishes like Boeuf Stroganoff— that's a steak embalmed in mushrooms.

LADY FITZADAM. Then I foresee you and the Vernons having a very happy time discussing new and exciting menus.

WILLIE. You really mean that?

LADY FITZADAM. I'm sure of it. Happy now?

WILLIE. Deliriously!

CORPORAL (*contemptuously*) Oogh! (*He moves to* L *of the table down* L *and busies himself with his paysheets*)

WILLIE. Forgive my little outburst, but when one lies in bed at night dreaming—(*he counts his notes*) five pounds—of new dishes . . .

LADY FITZADAM. The heart-burnings of the creative artist.

WILLIE. Exactly, madam. You're so wonderfully understanding.

LADY FITZADAM. Am I? Good. Well, that's all, Willie. (*She turns to the fireplace*)

(WILLIE *crosses to the doors up* C)

(*She turns*) Ask little Biddy to come in, will you?

WILLIE (*stopping and turning*) Biddykins?

CORPORAL. Gertcha!

(WILLIE *mouths something unprintable at the Corporal, then exits up* C, *closing the doors behind him*)

(*He suddenly remembers something and crosses to* C) Oh, yes. The Sergeant at the camp telephone exchange was asking if all our calls were to go on the official account or the General's private one.

LADY FITZADAM (*moving* RC) His private one, of course. And remember to remind me to charge them up on their bills.

CORPORAL. I hope the Sergeant isn't getting suspicious.

LADY FITZADAM. How do you mean?

CORPORAL. He said that last month all we had beside the local calls was one to London and two to Dorset.

LADY FITZADAM. Well?

CORPORAL. And this month, we've already had four to London,

three to Paris, two to New York and eleven to San Francisco.
LADY FITZADAM. You must explain to the Sergeant that they are
in connection with the General's mission, which is highly "top
secret", so he'd better keep his mouth shut. (*She turns away to the
fireplace*)

(*The* CORPORAL *moves to the table down* L.
BIDDY *peeps shyly in the door up* C, *then comes into the room. She
wears a striped housemaid's dress and a large white apron*)

CORPORAL. Biddy? Army pay. Sign here.

(BIDDY *moves down* L, *signs, takes her pay packet from the* CORPORAL
then moves up C. LADY FITZADAM *crosses to* L *of the sofa*)

LADY FITZADAM. Lolly. (*She hands Biddy five pounds*)
BIDDY. Five pounds!
LADY FITZADAM. Biddy, we've probably got some more guests
arriving.
BIDDY. American?
LADY FITZADAM. No. Why?
BIDDY. I like them. They're such fun. They make me laugh.
LADY FITZADAM. Well, I'm afraid these are English. You'd
better get the double spare room ready. (*She turns away*)
BIDDY. Yes, madam. (*She turns to go, stops, thinks a second, then turns
to Lady Fitzadam*) You don't think Mr Hoffman knows anything, do
you?
LADY FITZADAM (*turning*) How do you mean?
BIDDY. He keeps asking such awkward questions. How the
General—I mean, the Professor—was killed.
LADY FITZADAM. And what did you say?
BIDDY. That he was having a cup of tea and went "poof".
LADY FITZADAM. Exactly.
BIDDY. Then he saw the inscription on the clock. To Major and
Mrs Fitzadam on the occasion of their marriage.
LADY FITZADAM. Oh!
BIDDY. But I told him that your husband started in the Royal
Engineers and finished up a dead scientist.
LADY FITZADAM. Brilliant, Biddy.
BIDDY. But this morning, when I took Mr Hoffman in his cup of
tea, he was lying there talking to himself.
LADY FITZADAM. What about?
BIDDY. "It's her blonde hair", he said, "just like ma's used to
be".
CORPORAL (*moving to* L *of Biddy*) Don't tell me he's after Suzie,
too?
BIDDY (*demonstrating*) By the way he stroked it, it looked more
like madam's.
LADY FITZADAM. Mine?

CORPORAL. Well, you can tell him the greenhouse is full up. (*He moves to* L *of the table down* L)

LADY FITZADAM. That's quite enough of that, Mr Green. (*To Biddy*) And if he asks any more awkward questions . . .

BIDDY. I'll let you know, madam.

LADY FITZADAM. Thank you, Biddy. (*She moves to the fireplace*)

(BIDDY *exits up* C.
SAM *enters by the upstage french windows and crosses to the* L *of sofa*)

SAM. Could I have a word with you, ma'am?

LADY FITZADAM (*moving the cashbox to the table* R *of the sofa, out of Sam's view*) Yes, of course. Nothing wrong, I hope?

SAM (*moving below the left end of the sofa*) Yes and no.

(*The* CORPORAL *moves below the desk*)

That Mac—is he a reliable sort of guy?

LADY FITZADAM (*moving below the right end of the sofa*) As a chauffeur or on the river?

SAM. On the river.

LADY FITZADAM (*floundering*) His conduct sheet—his references— I mean, he has the reputation of being one of the finest ghillies in Scotland.

SAM. Not the sort to double-cross anyone?

LADY FITZADAM. Good heavens, no. Why do you ask?

SAM (*awkwardly*) It's just that—well, you see—whenever I'm watching Larry, he never catches a thing.

LADY FITZADAM. Well?

SAM (*looking at the Corporal*) But the moment my back is turned— a twenty-two pounder.

LADY FITZADAM. Mr Goulansky! You're not suggesting . . . ?

SAM. I'm not suggesting anything—just seems sort of strange.

LADY FITZADAM. Beginner's luck, I expect. Aren't you going to have a go yourself?

SAM. A little later, perhaps. When Larry's finished with Mac.

(LADY FITZADAM *turns away*.
SAM *moves to the Corporal, slips him a pound note then exits by the downstage french windows*)

CORPORAL (*crossing to Lady Fitzadam*) More for the kitty.

LADY FITZADAM (*taking the note*) What's this?

CORPORAL. For telling Suzie he's waiting in the greenhouse.

LADY FITZADAM (*holding out the note*) No, that's yours—personal services.

CORPORAL (*crossing to* LC) I wouldn't touch it.

LADY FITZADAM (*following the Corporal*) Oh, yes, you would.

CORPORAL. Well, if you insist. (*He takes the note and thrusts it into his trousers pocket*) All the same, if I had my way, I'd . . .

C

LADY FITZADAM. Try and control yourself, Mr Green, and never forget . . .

CORPORAL (*pointing to the motto*) I know, I know. "The customer is always right."

LADY FITZADAM. You'd better give Suzie his message. (*She returns to the fireplace*)

(*The* CORPORAL *moves to the doors up* C, *opens them and goes into the hall*)

CORPORAL (*calling*) Suzie. (*He comes into the room and closes the doors*)

LADY FITZADAM. And ask Huggins to come in, will you?

CORPORAL. It's his afternoon off.

LADY FITZADAM. When will he be back?

CORPORAL (*moving* C) God knows. He went up to the camp to draw his pay and have a couple at the canteen, then he said he was going down to the local.

LADY FITZADAM (*holding up five one-pound notes*) I'll give him these when he gets back. (*She picks up the cash-box, puts it on the firestool and puts the five pounds in it*)

CORPORAL. Just as well he hasn't got them now, or he might never get back at all.

(SUZIE *enters up* C *and moves down* C, *flashing the brooch she is wearing. The* CORPORAL *moves to the table down* L)

SUZIE. Smashing, isn't it?

LADY FITZADAM (*holding out five one-pound notes*) And here's your share.

SUZIE (*taking the notes*) Five! Must be my lucky day.

CORPORAL. Private Tidmarsh. Pay!

(SUZIE *stuffs the notes down her bosom and crosses to the table down* L. *The* CORPORAL *crosses to the stool.* SUZIE *signs*)

SUZIE (*picking up her pay packet*) Kid stuff! (*She puts the packet down her bosom*)

LADY FITZADAM. Mr Green has a message for you.

CORPORAL (*with his back to the audience*) Greenhouse!

SUZIE. Mr Goulansky?

(*The* CORPORAL *nods*)

(*She goes to the downstage french windows, then stops and turns*) Well, mustn't keep the customers waiting.

(SUZIE *laughs loudly and exits by the french windows*)

CORPORAL (*moving to the doors up* C) Martyrdom, that's what it is.

LADY FITZADAM (*holding out five one-pound notes*) Worth it, isn't it?

(*The* CORPORAL *stops, turns, crosses to Lady Fitzadam and takes the notes*)

CORPORAL. Maybe.

(LADY FITZADAM *moves below the right end of the sofa*)

Here, listen, if I have any luck with these paintings, can I keep ten per cent?

LADY FITZADAM. Those! You wouldn't sell them in a thousand years.

CORPORAL (*doggedly*) Ten per cent.

LADY FITZADAM. Very well.

(*The* CORPORAL *exits up* C, *closing the door behind him.* LADY FITZ-ADAM *puts the remaining five pounds in her bag, then hides the cash-box in the firegrate and replaces the firescreen.*

LARRY HOFFMAN *enters up* L *on the verandah, moves down and comes in by the downstage french windows. He is in his middle forties and is a real charmer. His soft voice and gracious manners are in direct contrast to Sam's vulgarities. He carries a fishing-rod and fishing bag*)

LARRY (*standing in the window*) Hello, there!

LADY FITZADAM (*turning*) Oh, hello, Mr Hoffman. Any more luck?

(LARRY *puts his fishing bag against the window and his rod beside the chest* L)

LARRY. After that twenty-two pounder? That'd be asking too much.

LADY FITZADAM (*moving below the left end of the sofa*) There's a cable for you on the desk. It came just after you'd gone out.

(LARRY *collects the cable from the desk, moves above the stool, throws his cap on to the stool, opens the cable and reads it. He then crosses to the telephone*)

LARRY (*indicating the telephone*) May I?

LADY FITZADAM. Why, of course. (*She goes to the table down* L, *collects the paysheets and account book and puts them in the desk drawer*)

(LARRY *lifts the receiver*)

LARRY (*into the telephone*) San Francisco, please . . . Douglas two-four-three-six-eight . . . That's right . . . Thanks. (*He replaces the receiver*) Funny thing, in the States we always have girls on the switchboard.

LADY FITZADAM (*moving* LC) We usually do here. But you know how it is—small highland exchange—wife's probably cooking the haggis.

LARRY. Must be cooking an awful lot of haggis—I've struck nothing but the husband so far. (*He moves to* L *of the sofa*)

LADY FITZADAM. Perhaps she's sick or something.

LARRY. Kind of strange how confusing accents can be. If you

hadn't told me, I'd sworn that voice belonged to one of your London Cockneys.

LADY FITZADAM (*quickly changing the subject*) Now, what would you like—a cup of tea, or a drink?

LARRY. Scotch on the rocks.

LADY FITZADAM (*crossing to the table* R *of the sofa and pressing the bell-push*) I might have guessed. (*She turns to Larry and indicates the cable*) Nothing serious, I hope?

LARRY. No, just ma wishing me many happies.

LADY FITZADAM. Your birthday?

LARRY (*moving* LC) Tell you the truth, I'd forgotten all about it. Seen Sam?

LADY FITZADAM. He went out ten minutes ago.

LARRY (*anxiously*) Fishing?

LADY FITZADAM. No, I think stalking.

LARRY. Stalking! That old stuff! (*He moves to the table down* L)

(*The* CORPORAL *enters up* C *carrying a tray with a bottle of whisky, a bottle of gin, a glass containing whisky and ice and a glass of gin and tonic. He moves to* R *of Larry, leaving the door open*)

LADY FITZADAM. Well done, Mr Green. You must have read my thoughts.

CORPORAL (*to Larry*) Scotch on the rocks, sir?

LARRY (*taking the glass of whisky and ice*) You read mine, too.

CORPORAL (*moving to Lady Fitzadam*) Gin and tonic, madam?

LADY FITZADAM (*taking the glass of gin and tonic*) Thank you.

(*The* CORPORAL *crosses and puts the tray and bottles on the table down* L. LARRY *moves to the doors up* C, *closes them then goes to the table* L *of the sofa and puts his glass on it*)

LARRY. Mind if I get something off my chest?

LADY FITZADAM. Why, of course not.

LARRY. It's just that I shouldn't like to see any of you nice folks getting into trouble—particularly on our account.

(*The* CORPORAL *transfers the bottles to the trolley* L, *and picks up the tray*)

LADY FITZADAM. Trouble?

(*The* CORPORAL *anxiously twirls the tray and tries to escape up* C)

LARRY. My dad always used to say, "If you've anything on your mind, get it off your chest." (*He intercepts the Corporal just in time*) Not leaving, Mr Green?

CORPORAL. I thought perhaps you'd rather discuss this alone.

LARRY. You stay right here. (*He leads the Corporal down* LC) You're in this just as much as she is. Maybe more. (*He turns up* C) Don't quite know how to say it, but I've a hunch—(*he moves down* C) that Sam Goulansky is getting sexy ideas about your Suzie.

LADY FITZADAM (*with a sigh of relief*) Fancy. (*She puts her glass on the table* R *of the sofa*)
LARRY (*moving above the stool*) Noticed anything, Mr Green?
CORPORAL (*moving to* L *of Larry*) Noticed anything . . .

(*The* CORPORAL *is about to continue when* LADY FITZADAM *moves to* R *of Larry and interrupts*)

LADY FITZADAM. I'm not surprised. A lot of our guests find her very attractive. Don't they, Mr Green?
CORPORAL (*with feeling*) They do.
LARRY. Let me know if he gives any trouble. Hell of a great guy —Sam. Got this one kink, though—sort of occupational neurosis. Chased girls all over the *Queen Mary*. Captain threatened to turn him off at Cherbourg.
CORPORAL (*moving to* R *of the table down* L) Pity he didn't.

(LADY FITZADAM *moves to* L *of the sofa*)

LARRY. Keep an eye open, Mr Green. Shouldn't like to see an innocent girl like that getting into trouble.
CORPORAL (*turning to Larry*) Trouble? Leave it to me, governor.
LARRY (*moving up* R *of the desk*) Life is so complex. Never quite sure what it's all about. Like these modern pictures. (*He looks at the paintings*) Can't sort of see what they're driving at.

(*The* CORPORAL *moves to* R *of Larry*)

CORPORAL (*to Larry; confidentially*) Zardeen!

(LADY FITZADAM *turns away to the fireplace and smiles*)

LARRY. How's that?
CORPORAL (*aside to Larry*) She doesn't know. Tell you later.

(*The* CORPORAL *exits up* C, *closing the doors behind him*)

LARRY (*moving* LC) What was all that about?
LADY FITZADAM (*moving to* R *of the sofa and picking up her drink*) No idea. (*She moves below the left end of the sofa*) Here's wishing you many happy returns, Mr Hoffman.
LARRY (*picking up his drink*) Of my birthday or being back here?
LADY FITZADAM. Why—both.
LARRY. Thanks. Though it would make it cosier if you called me "Larry".
LADY FITZADAM. That's very nice of you, but . . .
LARRY. Oh, I know what you're going to say. "Never mix business with pleasure" and all that old malarky. What about the oldest of them all, "The Customer is always right"?
LADY FITZADAM (*smiling and raising her glass*) Many happy returns—Larry.
LARRY. That's more like it. Won't you sit down?

(LADY FITZADAM *sits* C *of the sofa*)

(*He crosses and sits* R *of Lady Fitzadam on the sofa*) And what am I going to call you? So far, all I've heard is "Mrs Fitzadam" or "madam".

LADY FITZADAM. Rather a stupid name, I'm afraid—"Dorothy".

LARRY. Nothing stupid about "Dorothy". (*He puts his hand over hers*) I've got a sister called Dorothy. Back home she's always known as Dot or Dotty, but do you know what I call her?

(*The telephone rings.* LARRY *puts his glass on the table* R *of the sofa, and lifts the receiver with his right hand whilst still holding Lady Fitzadam's hand with his left*)

(*Into the telephone*) Thanks . . . That you, Ma? . . . This is Larry . . . Just called to thank you for the cable—never forget, Sweetheart, do you? . . . Older? . . . No, I'm feeling younger every day; and do you know what, Ma—I just caught a twenty-two pounder . . . (*In his enthusiasm he lifts Lady Fitzadam's arm high in the air*) No, a fish— the biggest that's ever been caught on this water . . . (*He laughs*) You didn't expect me to catch it on dry land? . . . Ma, you say the cutest things. And tell you another thing, Ma—this Scottish manse . . . No—M-A-N-S-E . . . Skip it, Ma—this stately home where Flora Macdonald once . . .

(LADY FITZADAM *struggles to free her hand*)

No, not Jeanette—Flora. This guest-house, Ma—I'm going to bring you here one day . . . Cold? . . . It's got central heating and steaks as good as—well, almost as good as you give me at home. And so many servants, you might be in the White House . . .

(LADY FITZADAM *manages to free her hand, and rises, only to be gripped around the waist by* LARRY, *who pulls her down on to the sofa and nearer to him*)

Listen, Ma. The lady who owns this manse—how I wish you could see her. She's kind of stately, but, Ma, when she smiles . . . What's that? . . . No, she's a widow . . . Why, of course I'm in love with her . . . Not yet. We're only at Christian names—and what do you think it is, Ma? . . . The same as you christened baby. So what do you think I'm going to call her? . . . That's right—"Dodo" . . . Well, there's the time check. Bye, bye, Sweetheart . . . Look after yourself. (*He replaces the receiver*) That was ma.

(LADY FITZADAM *tries to free herself*)

Don't move, Dodo. I know exactly what you're thinking. A guy on his vacation and out for a good time. You're so wrong. Remember that first time you talked to me on the telephone at the *Savoy?*

LADY FITZADAM. Only because I was so worried about your friend—Prawn Ffoulkes.

LARRY. Maybe, but that didn't stop me falling in love with your voice.

LADY FITZADAM. Now you're being absurd.
LARRY. What's absurd about that? I'm a man, aren't I? I've
a right to my feelings. Do you know I haven't felt like this since I
was a boy at college.

(LADY FITZADAM *manages to get free, rises, crosses to the table* R *of
the sofa and presses the bell-push.* LARRY *grabs her right wrist and pulls
her down again into the right corner of the sofa, leans over and smothers
her*)

LADY FITZADAM. Please, Mr Hoffman. Suppose one of the ser-
vants came in.
LARRY. To hell with the servants. Anyhow, they'd understand.
They're flesh and blood like us. (*Softly*) What's the good of resisting
it, Dodo? You and I didn't meet here by chance. Fate arranged it.
Kept us apart all these years, then suddenly brought us together.
(*He kisses her brow*) And don't you ever call me "Mr Hoffman"
again. (*He envelopes her and kisses her passionately*)

(*The* CORPORAL *enters up* C, *leaving the doors open. He stands
surprised by what he sees, then a broad grin breaks out on his face.* LADY
FITZADAM *tries to beckon the Corporal with her left hand to come to her
rescue, but the* CORPORAL *leans over the back of the sofa and mouths the
words: "The customer is always right."* LADY FITZADAM *shakes her fist
at him.*
The CORPORAL *exits quickly up* C, *closing the doors behind him.
The noise of the doors closing makes* LARRY *release Lady Fitzadam and
rise*)

What was that?

(LADY FITZADAM *jumps to her feet, goes to the fireplace and tidies her
hair*)

LADY FITZADAM. That was very naughty of you.
LARRY (*moving to her*) Dodo, darling . . .
LADY FITZADAM. No, I mean it. Just because I happen to run
a guest house, and you happen to be a wealthy visitor, you needn't
think . . .
LARRY. That's the unkindest thing you've ever said. And you're
going to take it back. (*He tries to kiss her*)

(LADY FITZADAM *pushes Larry aside and crosses to* LC)

LADY FITZADAM (*gesticulating*) What else am I to think? Dragging
me on to the sofa—using your brute strength—almost suffocating
me. Who do you think I am?
LARRY. I know perfectly well who you are. To the rest of the
world you are Mrs Fitzadam, but to me—(*he points to his heart*) and
that goes mighty deep—you're Dodo—the most gracious and lovely
lady I've met in years. (*He moves* RC) Just say "yes", Dodo, and no
matter where you want it—(*he moves* C) the States—Scotland—or

Timbuctoo—I'll give you the greatest little home in the world.

LADY FITZADAM (*moving to the armchair* LC; *desperately*) Larry, I don't want to seem ungrateful—please believe that—but honestly—this is all absurd. (*She moves to* L *of the chair*)

LARRY (*moving to* R *of the armchair* LC) Why?

LADY FITZADAM. I must go and get some flowers.

(LADY FITZADAM *rushes out by the downstage french windows.*
LARRY *follows her off. Immediately they have gone, the double doors up* C *burst open.*
The GENERAL *enters up* C. *He looks around and sees there is no-one in the room*)

GENERAL (*shouting*) Anyone at home? (*He lays his cap, stick and gloves on the upstage end of the desk, crosses to the table* R *of the sofa and rings the bell. As he goes he undoes his Sam Brown, takes it off and lays it over the desk chair. He sees Larry's fishing-rod, gingerly picks it up, holds it out into the room and tries the weight of it. He takes it out on to the verandah by the downstage french windows, holds it out over the parapet and swishes it*)

(*The* CORPORAL *tip-toes in up* C, *thinking Lady Fitzadam and Larry are still there. He sees they have gone and is about to exit when he sees the General and rushes off up* C. *The* GENERAL *hears the noise and comes into the room by the upstage french windows*)

What the blazes was that? (*He moves down* L, *replaces the fishing-rod and shouts*) Corporal!

CORPORAL (*off*) Sir!

GENERAL. Come here.

(*The* CORPORAL *rushes on up* C. *He is dressed in a complete suit of overalls and is doing up the buttons as he enters*)

CORPORAL (*standing to attention*) Sir!

GENERAL. Where've you been? Been pressing the bell all afternoon.

CORPORAL. Sorry, sir. I was outside cleaning out the coal shed, sir. I had to clear off, sir.

GENERAL. Oh.

CORPORAL. Nice to have you back, sir.

(*The* GENERAL *goes to the trolley and mixes himself a whisky and soda*)

GENERAL. Hell of a fine welcome this is. No car to meet me. Had to get a lift from the Air Force. No sentries at the gate. Where is everyone? Where's her Ladyship?

CORPORAL. I think she's gone up to the camp, sir.

GENERAL (*moving above the armchair* LC) What for?

CORPORAL (*suddenly inspired*) To see the Sergeant-Major's wife, sir. She's been taken queer, expecting twins.

GENERAL. Her ladyship?

CORPORAL. No, sir. The Sergeant-Major's wife.
GENERAL (*moving to the stool* C) Yes, stupid of me. Gave me quite
a turn. (*He picks up Larry's cap*) Whose is this? (*He examines the label in
the cap*) "Maynards, San Francisco."
CORPORAL (*nervously*) We've a couple of guests, sir.
GENERAL. Americans? (*He drops the cap on the stool*)
CORPORAL. Yes, sir.
GENERAL (*moving down* LC) Where are they?
CORPORAL. Fishing, sir.
GENERAL (*knowledgeably*) I thought that was an American rod.
I might have guessed. That damned War Office—always the same.
(*He moves to the desk*) Any official guests they don't know what to do
with—send them fishing—North-West District. (*He leans against the
desk and drinks*) General Fitzadam will look after them. Anyone'd
think this was a damned hotel.
CORPORAL (*weakly*) Yes, sir.
GENERAL (*moving up* C) Bring up my bags. Can't wait to get out
of this uniform.

(*The* GENERAL *exits up* C, *taking his drink with him. He leaves the
doors open. The* CORPORAL *rushes on to the verandah*)

CORPORAL (*calling*) Mrs Fitzadam! My lady!
GENERAL (*off; calling*) Corporal!

(*The* CORPORAL *dithers, puts his fingers to his mouth and whistles*)

(*Off; shouting*) Corporal!
CORPORAL (*calling*) Coming, sir.

(*The* CORPORAL *comes in by the downstage french windows and rushes
off up* C, *leaving the doors open.*
     LADY FITZADAM *and* LARRY *enter by the downstage french
windows.* LARRY *carries a bundle of greenery*)

LADY FITZADAM (*moving above the armchair* LC) Where is he?
LARRY. Who?
LADY FITZADAM. Mr Green. I thought I heard him calling. (*She
points to the table down* L) Put that down there, will you?
LARRY. Sure. (*He puts the greenery on the table down* L)

(LADY FITZADAM *notices the General's cap and stick on the desk and
picks them up*)

LADY FITZADAM. What on earth are these doing here?
LARRY (*crossing to* R *of Lady Fitzadam*) Looks like Sam must be
around.
LADY FITZADAM. Sam?
LARRY. You won't be sore, will you, Dodo? But Sam and I are
just zany Americans—laugh at crazy things.
LADY FITZADAM. I'm afraid I'm not with you.

LARRY. Sam found a lot of old junk like this in a cupboard in his room.

LADY FITZADAM. Oh, did he?

LARRY. It's that Huggins.

LADY FITZADAM. What about him?

LARRY. Beneath that rugged exterior there beats a heart aching to entertain the public. (*He takes the cap and cane from Lady Fitzadam and demonstrates Huggins wearing his props*) A wild craving to see his name in lights. Sam discovered it—Huggins just loves to perform.

LADY FITZADAM (*taking the cap and cane and replacing them on the desk*) Mr Green told me. And to think I've known him all these years and thought his only interests were pressing trousers and cleaning shoes.

LARRY. Take it from me, Dodo, he's a riot. That's why Sam and I have been sort of helping him. Trying to encourage his lust for histrionic expression. You should see Huggins all dressed up. He looks just great.

LADY FITZADAM (*moving to the table down L*) I bet he does.

LARRY (*following her*) You're not sore?

LADY FITZADAM. Of course not.

(LARRY *tries to kiss* LADY FITZADAM, *but she manages to evade him*)

Please, Larry. You promised outside that . . .

LARRY. And now I'm breaking that promise. Dodo, you're adorable.

LADY FITZADAM. Larry, please. (*She picks up the bundle of greenery and crosses to* RC)

LARRY (*following her with his eyes*) You can't stop me looking at you.

LADY FITZADAM. I suppose not.

LARRY. Look out!

LADY FITZADAM (*stopping*) What is it?

LARRY (*crossing to her*) Keep still—a caterpillar. (*He pretends to find it on her neck and is about to kiss her*)

(*The* GENERAL *enters up* C. *He has changed his uniform jacket for an old tweed one*)

GENERAL (*moving down LC*) Ah, there you are.

(LADY FITZADAM *spins around, hardly believing her eyes*)

LADY FITZADAM. Hamish!

GENERAL. Here I am. Safe and sound.

LADY FITZADAM. Ham—Ham—Hamish! (*She crosses slowly to him*)

GENERAL. Twins arrived yet?

LARRY (*taken aback*) What?

GENERAL. Not hers.

(LADY FITZADAM *looks in confusion from one to the other*)

LADY FITZADAM. Hamish—this is Mr Hoffman.

(*The* GENERAL *crosses to* L *of Larry and shakes hands*)

LARRY. Glad to know you, sir.

GENERAL. How do you do? Dodo been looking after you all right?

LARRY. You bet. You call her "Dodo", too?

GENERAL (*surprised*) Why, do you?

LADY FITZADAM (*quickly*) He has a sister called Dorothy and she has the same nickname.

GENERAL. I see. (*He moves above the table down* L *and indicates the fishing-rod*) That your rod?

LARRY. Sure is.

GENERAL. One of those new fibre-glass ones, isn't it?

LARRY. That's right.

(*The* GENERAL *goes to the rod, picks it up and examines it*)

(*He whispers to Lady Fitzadam*) Who's this?

LADY FITZADAM (*desperately*) My—my brother-in-law. (*She turns up* C)

GENERAL (*replacing the rod*) And very nice, too. (*He turns to Larry*) Been fishing yet?

LARRY. I'll say.

GENERAL. Any luck?

LARRY (*crossing to* LC) A twenty-two-pounder.

(LADY FITZADAM *puts the greenery on the table behind the sofa*)

GENERAL. A what?

LARRY. This very afternoon.

GENERAL. I don't believe it.

LARRY. You ask Mac.

GENERAL. Mac?

(LADY FITZADAM *moves to the door up* C *to try and warn the others*)

So that's why he wasn't there to meet me. (*He crosses to* L *of Lady Fitzadam*) You got my cable?

LADY FITZADAM. No, dear.

GENERAL. What?

LADY FITZADAM. No, dear.

GENERAL. Never mind. We can go into that later.

(LADY FITZADAM *turns to the doors up* C)

LADY FITZADAM. Yes. I'll just make sure your room is ready.

GENERAL. No hurry. (*He takes her left arm and turns her to face front*) What I really need is a Scotch and soda.

LADY FITZADAM. I'll go and fetch it. (*She turns to go*)

GENERAL. No need. There's some here.

(*The* General *takes* Lady Fitzadam's *other arm and swings her round. She crosses reluctantly to the trolley down* L *and pours a whisky and soda. The* General *closes the doors up* C *and moves down* LC)

Now, about that fish. Where were you fishing? (*He crosses to the fire-place*)

Larry. What's he call it? Monty's Meadow. (*He moves slightly* C)

General (*turning; amazed*) You don't mean it? Do you hear that, Dodo? Monty's Meadow. (*To Larry*) D'you know, I shudder to think the number of hours I must have spent fishing that stretch, and the most I ever got out of it is a ten-and-a-half-pounder and a grilse, and both long measly fish at that.

Larry. Sam's taken out three of over twenty.

General. Three? From Monty's Meadow?

Larry. Two from Monty's and one from what Mac calls Gort's Gulley. Your Scotch fishing grounds certainly have the cutest names.

(Lady Fitzadam *crosses to the General with the drink*)

Lady Fitzadam. Your drink, dear.

General (*taking the drink*) Three over twenty? It isn't possible.

Larry. You ask Mac.

(Lady Fitzadam *moves below the sofa*)

General. But that'd be good going on Lord Appleby's water, and that's the best in the west of Scotland. (*He turns to the fireplace and takes a swig at his drink*)

Larry (*moving to* L *of Lady Fitzadam*) Well, there it is. Maybe I'll go down and have another try before supper. (*He gives Lady Fitzadam a quick kiss and darts* L)

General (*turning*) Have a drink first?

Larry (*picking up his fishing-rod and bag*) No, thanks.

General (*crossing to* C) If I can, I'll come and join you later.

Larry (*moving to the downstage french windows*) That'll be great.

General (*raising his glass*) Tight lines. (*He drinks*)

Larry. Thanks.

(Larry *exits by the downstage french windows, passes along the verandah and exits up* L. *The* General *puts his glass on the upstage end of the table down* L *and turns with outstretched arms*)

General. At last, Dodo darling.

(Lady Fitzadam *moves to the General and embraces him. She pats him on the back with both hands, then changes arms over and does it again. The* General *breaks away, crosses to the table* R *of the sofa and presses the bell-push.* Lady Fitzadam *hurries to the doors up* C *to warn the others*)

Lady Fitzadam. Can I get you anything?

General (*moving to her; firmly*) You stay here. I've got lots to tell you.

(Lady Fitzadam *makes a final attempt to exit*)

LADY FITZADAM. Be back in a minute.
GENERAL (*irritably*) What's the matter, Dodo? (*He takes her arm and leads her down* C) You seem all on edge.
LADY FITZADAM. I'm fine.
GENERAL. Where's that damn Corporal?
LADY FITZADAM (*moving up* C) I'll get him.
GENERAL (*intercepting her*) Dodo, do relax. Get yourself a drink.
LADY FITZADAM (*sitting on the arm of the desk chair*) Yes.

(*The* GENERAL *crosses to the telephone and lifts the receiver*)

GENERAL (*to himself*) Three from Monty's . . . (*Into the telephone*) G.O.C. here—give me Signals . . . G.O.C. here. I sent a cable yesterday from the Azores. . . Not St. Mawes—Azores. Islands in the Pacific . . . all right, Atlantic then. What's it matter where they are . . . What matters is, why hasn't it arrived here? . . . you weren't on duty yesterday—well, get me someone who was. (*He slams down the receiver and moves above the sofa*) Damned Corporal. High time I got back, and gave 'em all a good shaking up.
LADY FITZADAM (*rising and moving up* C) Shall I?
GENERAL (*taking her arm and leading her down* C) You stay here. I'll deal with this in my own way. (*He crosses to the table down* L) Who is this Hoffman chap? All for Anglo-American relationship, of course, but when it comes to . . .

(*The* CORPORAL *enters up* C. *He is wearing his overalls. He stands* R *of Lady Fitzadam*)

CORPORAL. Sir.
GENERAL. You've been a hell of a long time.
CORPORAL. Sorry, sir.

(LADY FITZADAM *gathers courage, turns to look at the Corporal and finds to her amazement that he is in overalls. She staggers slightly down stage as if about to faint. The* GENERAL *turns to her and steadies her*)

GENERAL (*anxiously*) What's the matter, Dodo, are you all right?

(*The telephone rings*)

(*He crosses to the telephone and lifts the receiver. Into the telephone*) And about time, too . . .

(LADY FITZADAM *collapses on to the stool* C)

That's right, sent off yesterday—addressed to Lady Fitzadam . . . But, even if it only arrived at midday it should have been sent down here before now . . . Oh, I see . . . Right. (*He replaces the receiver. To the Corporal*) Tell Private Huggins I want to see him.
CORPORAL. Sorry, sir, it's his afternoon off.
GENERAL (*horrified*) Afternoon off?
CORPORAL (*swallowing and realizing his mistake*) I mean—he's got a late pass, sir.

GENERAL (*to Lady Fitzadam*) There you are, you see—there's the answer. I despatch a cable from the Azores, thousands of miles across oceans and continents. It's handled by people of every race and colour, most of 'em unable to speak a word of English. Does it get held up? Does it get lost? No! (*He crosses to the armchair* LC) Everything's fine until it reaches Headquarters, North-Western District. Then what happens? For the last few hundred yards of its journey, they entrust it to Private Huggins, probably the most unreliable man in the whole British Army. (*He picks up his glass, moves to the trolley, and refills it*) Half-way across the world in a matter of minutes at four and sevenpence a word, only to spend hour after hour in Private Huggins' pocket, propping up some four-ale bar. (*He squirts soda into his drink*) Dammit, it might have been something important—something requiring immediate action. (*He moves above the armchair* LC)

LADY FITZADAM (*rising and crossing to the table down* L) How right you are.

GENERAL (*moving to the Corporal*) Tell the rest of the staff I want to see them.

CORPORAL. Sir. (*He moves to the doors up* C)

GENERAL. Just as they are.

(*The* CORPORAL *turns and looks horrified at Lady Fitzadam, then exits up* C, *closing the doors behind him*)

Wait till I get hold of Huggins.

LADY FITZADAM. I shouldn't worry too much, dear. You're safely back—that's all that matters. But what went wrong? Why the early return?

GENERAL. I'd done a week at the nuclear plant in Texas—the place I wrote to you from. Lectures by long-haired scientists until my brain reeled with figures. (*He crosses with his drink to the fireplace*) Then on to Florida for high altitude flights with crew-cropped pilots until my brain reeled with oxygen and outer space. Then— a wreck mentally and physically—what happens?

LADY FITZADAM (*moving* C) I've no idea.

GENERAL. All further tests cancelled until after the Summit Conference. Can you beat it? (*He puts his glass on the mantelpiece*)

LADY FITZADAM. So you caught the next plane home?

GENERAL. Via the Azores.

CORPORAL (*off*) Left, right, left right . . .

LADY FITZADAM. Such a lovely surprise. (*She plucks up courage*) Darling, there's one little thing I think I ought to explain . . .

(*The doors up* C *open.*

BIDDY, WILLIE *and the* CORPORAL *march on up* C. WILLIE *and the* CORPORAL *wear overalls and* BIDDY *is in an overall with a duster round her head. All three look dishevelled*)

CORPORAL. Left, right, left, right . . .

(BIDDY, *as she marches in, pushes* LADY FITZADAM *down stage.*

LADY FITZADAM *finally sits in the chair below the table down* L)
Parade halt. Right turn. Stand at ease.

(*The* GENERAL *crosses to* C)

We were all in the coal shed, sir.
GENERAL. Good afternoon.
WILLIE. Good afternoon and welcome back, sir.
GENERAL. Who's missing?
CORPORAL. Huggins, sir.
GENERAL. I know all about him.
CORPORAL. And Private Tidmarsh, sir. She's up at the Naafi, sir.
GENERAL (*moving to the fireplace*) Oh. (*He collects his drink*) Well, I just wanted to see how you all were. No complaints during my absence?
CORPORAL. Far from it, sir.
GENERAL. Good. (*He moves* RC) Afraid you've had these official guests to contend with. Oh, and that reminds me, Private Maltravers . . .

(WILLIE *steps forward two paces and stands to attention*)

While I was in America I've eaten nothing but . . .
WILLIE. I know, sir—steaks.
GENERAL. Dead right, Maltravers. So I thought that tonight for a change . . .
WILLIE. Might I suggest a nice little shishkababah?
GENERAL (*looking in horror at Willie*) Suppose we say a couple of nice kippers and some scrambled eggs. (*He turns away and sips his drink*)
WILLIE. Very good, sir. (*He steps back into line*)
GENERAL. That's all for now. (*He moves to the fireplace and turns*) And thank you for your loyal support to her laydship during my absence.
CORPORAL. Been a pleasure, sir. (*He steps forward, moves down a little and faces Willie and Biddy. As he does so, he hisses to Willie in disgust*) Shsihicababah! (*To both of them*) Parade shun.

(LADY FITZADAM *rises and looks out front*)

Right turn, quick march. Left, right, left, right.

(WILLIE *and* BIDDY *march out up* C. *The* CORPORAL, *keeping in step, moves to* R *of Lady Fitzadam, and marks time whilst speaking to her in a loud whisper*)

Have you told him?
LADY FITZADAM. Not yet.
CORPORAL. What do we wear?
LADY FITZADAM. One ring—civvies. Two rings—khaki.

CORPORAL. Trousers and all?
LADY FITZADAM. Of course.

(*The* CORPORAL *turns and marches off up* C, *closing the doors behind him*)

(*She moves below the desk*) As I was saying, darling—about your house in Dorset . . .
GENERAL. Ah, talking of houses, that reminds me. (*He moves* RC) Most extraordinary thing happened. I had a letter from the War Office . . .
LADY FITZADAM. War Office? What about?
GENERAL. This place.
LADY FITZADAM (*anxiously*) Anything wrong?
GENERAL. Everything wrong. Sit down. (*He goes to her and leads her to the sofa*)

(LADY FITZADAM *crosses below the General and sits on the sofa at the left end*)

Completely shattered my whole faith in human nature. I mean it, Dodo. (*He crosses and sits* R *of Lady Fitzadam on the sofa*) It's nearly forty years since I went to Sandhurst. Forty years during which I like to think I've served the colours to the best of my ability.
LADY FITZADAM. You're absolutely right.
GENERAL. Taking it all round, a career, I think, most people would be proud of.
LADY FITZADAM. And justly so.
GENERAL. With every right to look forward to a pension honourably earned.
LADY FITZADAM (*anxiously*) Hamish, they're not making trouble?
GENERAL. Making? They've made it. The War Office wrote to me—airmailed it to Florida. (*He leans over and presses the bell-push once*)

(LADY FITZADAM *winces at the thought of the staff arriving in civvies*)

Dodo, I could hardly believe my eyes. I'm telling you, Dodo, I found this most upsetting. (*He rises and moves to the fireplace*) To finish a long and distinguished career on what amounts to nothing less than a slur on my integrity. (*He drinks*) How dare they suggest that . . . (*He moves to the table* R *of the sofa and presses the bell-push twice*) Where's that damned Corporal?

(LADY FITZADAM *breathes a sigh of relief that he has rung twice*)

(*He crosses to the desk*) You wait till you read this letter. You'll feel just as insulted as I do.
LADY FITZADAM. Was it from anyone special?
GENERAL. The War Minister, himself—personal.
LADY FITZADAM (*rising and moving to* L *of the sofa*) Darling, there's something I *must* explain.

GENERAL (*rising*) In a moment. (*He rises, moves up* c *and calls*) Corporal!

CORPORAL (*off*) Coming, sir.

GENERAL (*moving down* L) Lot of damn Civil Servants. Nothing better to do than go snooping around.

(LADY FITZADAM *sits on the sofa at the left end. The* CORPORAL *enters up* c, *buttoning his overalls*)

CORPORAL (*moving* c) Sir.

GENERAL. You've been a hell of a long time.

CORPORAL. Sorry, sir. Went back to finish off the coal shed, sir. Had to clean off, sir.

GENERAL. Well, stop worrying about the coal, and pay more attention to me.

CORPORAL. Sir!

GENERAL. At the bottom of my suitcase, there's a large brown envelope. Bring it down, will you?

CORPORAL. Sir.

(*The* CORPORAL *exits up* c, *closing the doors behind him*)

LADY FITZADAM. Now, Hamish, you really must listen.

GENERAL. One thing at a time, my dear. (*He moves down* L) You wait till you read this letter. I was so upset—so angry. D'you know, I felt quite sick.

(*The telephone rings*)

(*He crosses to the telephone and lifts the receiver. Into the telephone*) Who? . . . Yes, she's here. (*He holds out the receiver*) It's for you, my dear.

(LADY FITZADAM *rises to take the receiver*)

Someone called "Vernon".

(LADY FITZADAM *reacts to the name, then takes the receiver*)

Why people still call you "Mrs Fitzadam" beats me. (*He crosses to the armchair* LC *and sits*) Well over a year since I got my "K".

LADY FITZADAM (*into the telephone*) Hello . . . Yes, speaking . . . Oh, hello, Mr Vernon . . . (*She glances anxiously at the General*) Oh, I am so glad. Tell your wife not to worry—to come as soon as she can . . . No trouble at all . . . We can always knock up a little something . . . Good-bye. (*She replaces the receiver*)

GENERAL. Who the devil are the Vernons?

LADY FITZADAM (*hopelessly*) I don't know.

GENERAL. Then why are they coming here? (*He rises*) More of these damn official guests, I suppose. Really, dear, this is too much.

LADY FITZADAM (*crossing to* R *of him*) Now listen, Hamish. Your house in Dorset . . .

GENERAL. Gundog Manor? What about it?

LADY FITZADAM. Well, you see, knowing how much you wanted to retire there, I . . .

D

(*The* Corporal *enters up* c, *leaving the door open. He carries a large Army envelope*)

Corporal (*moving to* r *of Lady Fitzadam*) This the one, sir?
General (*taking the envelope*) That's it. (*He crosses to* rc)
Lady Fitzadam (*crossing to* l *of the General*) Now, once and for all, Hamish . . .

(*The* General *sits on the sofa at the right end and empties the letters from the envelope on to the floor*)

General. Just a minute, my dear. All very well to talk about retiring. You wait until you read this.

(Lady Fitzadam *slumps on to the sofa,* l *of the General. The* Corporal *stands* lc *with his back to the windows.*
Suzie *minces in by the downstage french windows. She is now wearing two brooches*)

Suzie (*moving below the desk*) Look what I've got.

(*The* Corporal *turns quickly and tries to hide Suzie from the General. She does not realize the situation and points to the Corporal's overalls*)

What are you all dressed up for?
General (*selecting a letter from the pile on the floor*) Ah, here it is.

(Suzie *looks round the Corporal, sees the General and freezes to attention. At the same time, the* General *sees Suzie, but as this is the first time she has been seen by him not wearing uniform, he does not recognize her*)

Good evening, my dear. (*To Lady Fitzadam*) You didn't tell me they'd brought their families. (*He rises, crosses to Suzie and shakes hands with her*)

(Suzie *backs away in fright. The* Corporal *backs up* l *in amazement*)

How do you do? Just back from the States myself.

(Sam *enters by the upstage french windows and stops on seeing the Corporal*)

Sam (l *of the Corporal*) Someone declared war?
General (*to Sam*) Tell me, this your daughter?
Sam (*with a wink*) You kidding? (*He moves to Suzie*)

(Suzie *moves behind the table down* l)

General. Oh, I see. Enjoying yourself, I hope?
Sam. I'll say. A twenty-pounder this morning. I just can't believe it. I keep looking around for my harp. (*To Lady Fitzadam*) Where's Larry?
General. Mr Hoffman? He's fishing.

SAM. The big heel!

(SAM *rushes out by the downstage french windows, passes along the verandah and exits up* L)

GENERAL. Great enthusiasts, these Americans. (*He crosses to* R *of the sofa*)

(*The* CORPORAL *makes frantic signals to Suzie.*
  SUZIE *runs out up* C.
The CORPORAL *follows Suzie off, closing the doors behind him*)

(*He flourishes the letter*) Now, listen to this. (*He reads*) "Dear Sir Hamish, forgive me for dealing with this on a personal basis, but it is obviously a matter of some embarrassment to the junior members of my staff." (*He picks up his glass from the mantelpiece and drinks*)

LADY FITZADAM. Go on.

GENERAL (*reading*) "Regarding your request for Service transport for removal of your personal belongings on retirement, I must point out that according to Army Regulations, clause eighty-three, para eighteen—(*he sips his drink*) only Service officers moving from one posting to another may make use of Service transport. (*He crosses to the table down* L) This does not apply, therefore, to a retiring officer moving to his civilian residence." (*He drains his glass, puts it on the table down* L, *then moves to the desk*) This writing-table—ours. (*He moves up* C) Those chairs—the sideboard in the dining-room—the dressing-table in the spare room—the pictures—the beds—all ours. Brought up here to the ends of the earth—and what for? So that the War Office could send their official guests to wear them out for us.

LADY FITZADAM. Too bad, my dear.

GENERAL. And yet, because this is a retiring job, they won't raise one finger to help us get the stuff back to civilization. I'm telling you, Dodo, this is an outrage. A damned outrage! (*He leans over the left end of the sofa*) Forty years of loyal service, and this is all the gratitude . . .

LADY FITZADAM (*rising*) Yes, yes, my dear.

GENERAL. Before I went abroad you made some highly immoral suggestions. This Ministry of Works carpet, for instance. You suggested replacing it with a cheaper one and pocketing the difference.

LADY FITZADAM. Only because I was so worked up about the house.

GENERAL. How much extra were they asking for the house?

LADY FITZADAM. A thousand. Why?

GENERAL. Then you shall have it. (*He gets more angry*) Change the carpet—sell your flowers and vegetables—flog the Army lawn-mower—the cultivator—the lot. (*With sudden fiendish joy*) Tell you what—set fire to the empty toolshed and I'll sign a form certifying that everything was inside.

LADY FITZADAM (*unbelieving*) You mean—work a little fiddle?

GENERAL (*throwing the letter into the air*) If that's the way they want it, it's a game two can play. (*He crosses to the trolley down* L)

LADY FITZADAM. What we need, darling, is a drink.

GENERAL (*picking up a whisky bottle*) Bottle's empty. (*He calls*) Corporal!

LADY FITZADAM (*calling*) Mr Green!

The CORPORAL *enters up* C *and moves down* C. *He is wearing an overall jacket over his black pin-striped trousers. The* GENERAL *and* LADY FITZADAM *burst out laughing. The* CORPORAL *looks down, realizes what he has done and reacts in horror as—*

the CURTAIN *falls*

ACT III

SCENE—*The same. Later that evening.*

When the CURTAIN *rises, the stage is empty. The lights are on and the french windows and curtains are open. It is bright moonlight outside. Empty coffee-cups are still about, giving the impression that dinner has not long finished. After a moment,* WILLIE *and* BIDDY *stroll arm in arm outside the french windows. They come into the room by the upstage windows and stand embracing.* WILLIE *is still wearing his chef's uniform, but* BIDDY *has changed into a smart maid's uniform. Whilst they embrace, the* CORPORAL *enters up* C, *closing the doors behind him. He is wearing a tail suit and black bow tie, and carries an ash-collector.*

CORPORAL. For heaven's sake, now you two at it. What is this—a monkey-house?

(BIDDY *moves quickly to* L *of the Corporal and displays an engagement ring on her finger*)

BIDDY. Look!
CORPORAL. Not you and Willie?
BIDDY. Isn't it gorgeous?
CORPORAL. Smashin'. Congratulations, son.

(WILLIE *moves to* L *of Biddy and shakes hands with the Corporal*)

WILLIE. Thank you very much.
CORPORAL. When are you going to get spliced?
WILLIE. Depends on what happens. If we go on taking in guests, we shall have saved enough by the autumn.
BIDDY. But if we have to go back to the Army . . .
CORPORAL (*moving to the table* RC) Just the way I was thinking. (*He empties the ashtray into his ash-collector*)
BIDDY (*moving below the sofa*) You? Not you and Suzie?

(*The* CORPORAL *moves to the door up* R, *opens it a little and looks off. The noise of a bridge game can be heard drifting in.* WILLIE *wanders down* L)

CORPORAL (*closing the door*) Beats me what's come over the General (*He points to the doors up* C) When I came in through that door and sees him standing there, then bolts and hears him shouting "Corporal" like blue murder, I'd have laid a hundred nicker to a Naafi rissole we'd all finish up the day in irons awaiting court martial. (*He empties the ashtray on the table* L *of the sofa*)
WILLIE. It's his loyalty to Dodo, that's what it is. (*He crosses below the Corporal to* L *of Biddy and puts his arm around her*) Who knows, Biddykins, one day I might have to do the same for you.

CORPORAL. Loyalty my foot! He's having the time of his life. There he is pretending he's a Colonel and playing the brother-in-law as if it was all his own idea. (*He moves to the table down* L *and empties the ashtray*) And by the looks on their faces, he's keeping up the old family tradition, and fleecing them good and hard.

WILLIE (*moving to* L *of the sofa*) But how can he get away with being a General up at the camp and a Colonel down here?

CORPORAL (*turning below the door down* L) All fixed. He's going to keep his uniform in the spare gardener's cottage, and change on the way up and down.

(SUZIE *enters up* C, *closing the door behind her. She is wearing a smart, maid's uniform*)

SUZIE (*moving* C *and showing off her two brooches*) Smashing, aren't they?

CORPORAL (*moving to* L *of Suzie*) Just a Jezebel, that's all you are.

SUZIE. A what?

CORPORAL. A gold-digger. Look at Biddy. She's got something worth a hundred of all your flashy stuff.

SUZIE. What?

CORPORAL. Show her, Biddy.

(SUZIE *crosses to* L *of* BIDDY *who displays her ring*)

SUZIE (*delighted*) Biddy! Willie?

(BIDDY *nods*)

(*She throws her arms around Biddy and kisses her*) But, Biddy, this is wonderful.

CORPORAL (*crossing to the door up* R) Shhhhhhh! (*He opens the door, peers off for a moment, then closes the door and moves to the fireplace*)

SUZIE. They can go to hell. Biddy and Willie are engaged. That's all that matters. Come on—let's drink their health. (*She crosses to the trolley*)

(*The front-door bell rings*)

CORPORAL (*crossing below the sofa to the doors up* C) Look out—that must be the new guests. Get those coffee things out of the way—quick.

(BIDDY *collects two empty coffee-cups from the table* RC)

SUZIE (*stubbornly*) But I want to drink Biddy's health.

CORPORAL. We'll do that later.

(*The* CORPORAL *exits up* C, *leaving the doors open.* BIDDY *crosses to the table down* L *and puts the cups on the coffee tray, then collects two cups from the table* L *of the sofa and puts them on the tray*)

WILLIE. Perhaps I'll be able to flog some of that salmon. I'll make such a lovely mayonnaise.

SUZIE (*to Biddy*) Well, just fancy—of course, I knew he was gone
on you. Anyone could see that. But somehow I never thought he
was the marrying sort.
WILLIE (*bashfully*) Neither did I.
SUZIE. When did you buy the ring? Today?
WILLIE. Just before the General went away. Then with all this
upheaval—all these guests, and so on—things seem to have changed.
SUZIE. You're telling me.

(*Voices are heard off up* c)

WILLIE. Look out, they're coming in here. (*He moves to* R *of the
doors up* c)

(BIDDY *moves and stands* L *of the doors up* c. SUZIE *crosses and picks
up the coffee tray.*
      The CORPORAL *enters up* c *and stands to one side.*
      LORD VERNON—PRAWN FFOULKES—*enters up* c. *He has both
the arrogance of the aristocrat and the astute mind of an experienced
politician. He wears a smart tweed suit*)

CORPORAL (*moving below the sofa*) This is the drawing-room, sir.
PRAWN (*moving down* c *and looking around*) And very nice, too.

(BIDDY *exits up* c, *leaving the doors open.*
      SUZIE *exits up* c *with the coffee tray, waggling her bottom as she
passes the Prawn*)

(*He turns and watches Suzie exit*) Very, very nice. (*He moves* LC)

(WILLIE *moves to* L *of the sofa*)

WILLIE. Will the gentleman be requiring any supper?
PRAWN (*taken aback*) At this time of night? Well, really, that's very
kind. If you could manage a sandwich or . . .
WILLIE (*with a step towards the Prawn*) Might I suggest—Merluche
à la Savoie—haddock with a poached egg and asparagus tips under
a creamed cheese sauce?
CORPORAL. With perhaps half a bottle of Bollinger?
PRAWN. But this is fantastic—in a guest-house in this country?
The perfect meal.
WILLIE. Thank you very much, sir.
CORPORAL. And your wife, sir?
PRAWN (*crossing to the fireplace*) No, she won't want anything. She'll
be going straight to bed. (*He turns to the Corporal*) Perhaps on second
thoughts—a little nightcap in her room.
CORPORAL. Champagne, sir?
PRAWN. What better?
CORPORAL. Leave it to me, sir. (*He turns to Willie*) That'll be all,
Chef, thank you.
WILLIE. Pleasure's mine.

(WILLIE *exits up* c, *closing the doors behind him*)

CORPORAL (*moving up* R *of the sofa*) I'll tell madam you're here, sir. She's playing bridge.

PRAWN. No hurry. (*He turns and looks at the picture on the wall below the fireplace*) This is rather gay.

CORPORAL (*moving below the right end of the sofa*) Zardeen!

PRAWN (*turning*) I beg your pardon?

CORPORAL (*with a step towards him*) The famous Zardeen, sir.

PRAWN. Never heard of him. (*He gestures to the telephone*) Can I put through a call? (*He moves to the table* R *of the sofa*)

CORPORAL. Certainly, sir. (*He moves towards the telephone*) Shall I?

PRAWN (*lifting the receiver*) Don't worry. (*Into the telephone*) Oban three-eight-four, please . . . (*Surprised*) You'll ring? . . . That's very kind of you. Thanks. (*He replaces the receiver and sits on the sofa at the right end*)

CORPORAL (*anxiously*) You're not an art dealer by any chance, sir?

PRAWN. Good heavens, no. Know nothing about it. Just know the sort of picture I like.

CORPORAL (*relieved*) Not surprised you haven't heard of Zardeen. (*He moves down* L *of the sofa*) Poor chap was killed—fell down a precipice . . .

PRAWN. Too bad.

CORPORAL (*moving to the desk chair*) So there's only a few of his picture's in existence. Madam's very lucky to have five of them. We had an art dealer here not long ago—a Mr Smith. Do you know what he did?

PRAWN. No idea.

CORPORAL. Came down one night when everyone was asleep. (*He indicates the lower picture over the desk*) Took this picture out of its frame, and do you know what he found written on the back?

PRAWN. Zardeen!

CORPORAL (*snapping his fingers*) Got it in one, sir.

PRAWN (*rising*) Why didn't he buy them?

CORPORAL (*moving to* L *of him*) Couldn't, sir. Not right away. You see, madam has no idea they're that valuable, so he couldn't let on, 'cos being an art dealer . . .

PRAWN (*crossing below the Corporal to the desk chair*) She'd get suspicious and put up the price?

CORPORAL (*moving to* R *of him*) Exactly, sir. So he left it to me to use my loaf and get 'em for fifty quid apiece.

PRAWN. And have you?

CORPORAL. It's kind of awkward, sir. (*He takes a couple of steps towards the door up* R, *pause, returns and speaks confidentially*) There's an American gentleman staying here who spotted them immediately. Seems to know all about pictures. He's offered me sixty.

(*The telephone rings*)

PRAWN (*moving to the telephone*) Ah! (*He lifts the receiver*)

CORPORAL. I'll put your wine on ice.

(*The* CORPORAL *exits up* C, *closing the doors behind him*)

PRAWN (*into the telephone*) Could I speak to . . . ? Oh, that you, sweetheart? . . . (*He sits on the sofa at the right end*) How's everything? . . . Yes, I'm at the guest-house now. Fantastic place. Nothing too much trouble. You'll adore it. How long will you be? . . . (*He glances at his watch*) Well, get rid of 'em as soon as you can . . . See you soon. (*A sudden afterthought*) Oh, and, sweetheart—just in case I'm not at the front door to meet you, you'd better be very tired and have a bad headache and go straight to bed. . . But, sweetheart, we don't want to sit up all night gossiping to a lot of strangers . . . Yes, there'll be a nice bottle of champagne waiting in the bedroom. And I've got you a birthday present. (*He taps his pocket*) Something you'll adore. Bye-bye. (*He replaces the receiver, takes out his spectacles, puts them on, then takes a notebook from his pocket and looks up a telephone number. He lifts the receiver. Into the telephone*) Trunks, please . . . That's very kind of you . . . Whitehall nine-four-double-o . . . You'll ring . . . Thanks. (*He replaces the receiver, rises, crosses to the desk, looks towards the doors up* C *then leans over the desk, takes hold of the lower picture and tries to look behind it*)

(*The* CORPORAL *enters up* C, *closing the door behind him.* PRAWN *hastily releases the picture, leaving it askew*)

CORPORAL. Supper won't be long, sir.
PRAWN. Good. (*He crosses to the fireplace*) Very attentive exchange. Insist on doing the calls for you. (*He removes his spectacles*)
CORPORAL (*moving to* L *of the sofa*) A special arrangement for our guests, sir. You'd find it very different if you rang up from anywhere else.
PRAWN. That's real service if you like. Far too rare these days. (*He puts on his spectacles, turns and looks at the picture down* R)

(*The* CORPORAL *adjusts the picture over the desk*)

You say the art dealer was offering sixty?
CORPORAL. That's right, sir.
PRAWN (*moving to* L *of the sofa*) Zardeen? Yes, I seem to remember the name. I'll make it sixty-five.

(LADY FITZADAM *enters up* R *and comes down* C. *She wears an evening gown. The* PRAWN *moves below the sofa. The* CORPORAL *stands above the armchair* LC)

LADY FITZADAM. I thought I heard voices. Mr Vernon?

(PRAWN *nods and shakes hands with Lady Fitzadam*)

(*She turns to the Corporal*) Mr Green, you should have let me know.
PRAWN. My fault entirely. I asked him not to disturb the bridge.

Lady Fitzadam. Just a friendly game. Ten shillings a hundred. Your wife not here yet?

Prawn. No. She's visiting some dreary relations in Oban. I told her to come along as soon as she could.

Lady Fitzadam. I see.

Prawn. So, in the meantime—aided and abetted by your *maître d'hôtel* and your very persuasive chef—I've fallen for a *recherché* little meal.

Corporal (*moving to the doors up* c) I'll see if it's ready, sir.

Lady Fitzadam (*moving above the armchair*) Splendid—splendid! You'd better serve it in the morning-room, Mr Green. It will be quieter.

Corporal. Yes, madam.

(*The* Corporal *exits up* c)

Prawn (*moving* c) If I may say so, Mrs Fitzadam, this is the most remarkable establishment.

Lady Fitzadam. I do hope you'll be comfortable. What are they giving you for supper?

Prawn. Merluche à la Savoie. Sounds delicious.

Lady Fitzadam (*crossing down* r *of the sofa*) Chef will be delighted. He made it as a speciality for dinner, but some of our guests preferred red meat.

Prawn (*turning to her*) Then their loss is my gain.

General (*off; calling*) Come on, Dodo. Your deal.

Lady Fitzadam (*moving to the door up* r) Will you excuse me? I'll just finish the rubber.

Prawn. Yes, of course.

Lady Fitzadam. Thank you. I won't be long.

Prawn. Don't hurry, please.

(Lady Fitzadam *exits up* r. Prawn *looks around at the pictures, strolls to the downstage french windows and goes on to the terrace.* Suzie *enters up* c, *closes the doors, moves to the left end of the sofa and puts the cushions tidy. She moves along the sofa to the right end. As she bends over the right end and thumps a cushion,* Prawn *enters by the upstage french windows and coughs.* Suzie *straightens up with a start*)

Suzie. Your supper's ready, sir.

Prawn (*moving* c) That's very quick.

Suzie. Willie—I mean chef—thought you'd like to start off with melon.

Prawn. Can't think of anything nicer. (*He moves to* l *of Suzie*) And what's your name, my dear?

Suzie. "Suzie", sir.

Prawn. Suzie? How very nice. (*He suddenly catches sight of Suzie's brooches*) So that's who they were for.

Suzie. How do you mean?

Prawn. American gentleman?

SUZIE. That's right, sir.

PRAWN (*crossing to the desk chair*) I met him in the shop when he was buying them. It was he who recommended me to come here.

SUZIE. Sam? Mr Goulansky?

PRAWN. Obviously a man of taste.

SUZIE. Bit of all right, aren't they?

PRAWN (*sitting on the edge of the desk*) I was thinking more of the—ah—recipient.

SUZIE. You mean me?

(PRAWN *takes a small box from his pocket and displays a brooch*)

PRAWN. I was buying this at the time.

SUZIE (*crossing to* C) Smashing! For your wife?

PRAWN. Er—yes. (*He rises*)

SUZIE. Just as well Mr Goulansky left his in New York.

PRAWN (*leaning over the desk chair to Suzie*) You're a very clever girl, Suzie.

(*The* CORPORAL *enters up* C. *He sees that Suzie is up to her old tricks*)

CORPORAL (*firmly*) Supper is served, sir.

PRAWN (*moving to the doors up* C) Thank you.

(SUZIE *moves towards the doors up* C. PRAWN *turns and looks at Suzie*)

CORPORAL. Straight through, sir.

PRAWN. Thank you.

(PRAWN *exits up* C. SUZIE *is about to follow but the* CORPORAL *grabs her arm*)

CORPORAL. You leave him alone. His wife'll be here any minute.

SUZIE. I didn't do anything. He started it, not me.

CORPORAL. I don't care who started it. (*He moves to* R *of the desk chair*) You'll be giving the place a bad name.

SUZIE (*moving to* R *of the Corporal*) Jealous, that's what you are.

CORPORAL (*turning to her*) Of course I'm jealous. (*He moves to* R *of the table down* L) How would you like it if you was in love with someone and every time they came round the corner you saw them making eyes at somebody else.

SUZIE (*moving to* R *of him*) Did you say "love", Moonshine?

(*Voices are heard off up* R)

CORPORAL. Look out! (*He pushes Suzie away slightly*)

(LADY FITZADAM *and* SAM *enter up* R. SAM *is wearing dinner clothes.* SUZIE *takes this opportunity to exit up* C. *The licentious* SAM *tries to stop her, but* SUZIE *is too quick for him*)

LADY FITZADAM. Mr Vernon all right?

CORPORAL. Having his supper, madam.

LADY FITZADAM. Good. (*To Sam*) Make yourself at home—I'll be back in a minute. (*She moves to the door up* c) Just some egg sandwiches, Mr Green.

CORPORAL. Certainly, madam. (*He moves towards the doors up* c)

(SAM *intercepts the Corporal and holds out a pound note*)

SAM (*greedily*) Greenhouse.

CORPORAL. No!

LADY FITZADAM. Mr Green!

> (*The* CORPORAL *reluctantly takes the note.*
> LADY FITZADAM *exits up* c.
> *The* CORPORAL *follows her off, closing the doors behind him.* SAM
> *crosses to the upstage french windows and looks out.*
> LARRY *and the* GENERAL *enter up* R. LARRY *wears a white tuxedo.*
> *The* GENERAL *is in dinner clothes and is counting some notes*)

LARRY (*moving to the fireplace*) I've been to the cleaners.

GENERAL (*moving above the sofa*) Sorry you've had such bad luck. (*He stuffs the notes into his pocket*) Perhaps, next time . . . Mr Goulansky —a cigarette.

SAM. No, thanks. Think I'll take a stroll. What a night. Take a look at that full moon. I think I'll just take a stroll.

(LARRY *darts to Sam, takes his arm and draws him* LC)

LARRY. I know you're moon crazy and all that, but just remember we're not at home—we're guests in someone else's house.

SAM. Are you talking about dames or fish?

LARRY. Well . . .

SAM. Tomorrow should be a great day.

LARRY. Tomorrow?

SAM. For salmon.

(SAM *exits hurriedly by the downstage french windows*)

LARRY (*moving* c) I didn't like the sound of that—didn't like it at all.

GENERAL. How do you mean?

LARRY (*moving* L *of the sofa*) Oh, he's a hell of a nice guy—Sam, but sort of unstable at times.

GENERAL (*moving* R *of the sofa*) You mean with the opposite sex?

LARRY (*shaking his head*) That's just a disease—something to do with his glands.

(*The* GENERAL *sits on the sofa at the right end*)

(*He moves to the table down* L *and leans against it*) No, Sam was brought up in a tough school of business—every man for himself. You know what I mean?

GENERAL. I think so.

LARRY. And it's become a kind of fixation. He's just *got* to win.

GENERAL. Win what?

LARRY. Anything he takes on. Guess I shouldn't be talking like this behind his back, but we made a bet when we came up here—who'd catch the most fish, see?

GENERAL. And he's leading?

LARRY. He certainly is. But what beats me is—how does he catch them? (*He moves below the table down* L)

GENERAL. Perhaps you're not using the right fly.

LARRY (*moving to* L *of the sofa*) It's nothing to do with flies. How come he's never caught a fish when I'm watching—never looked like catching one? Now, tomorrow morning it's his turn with Mac . . . Don't think I'm suggesting anything.

GENERAL. Of course not.

LARRY. But I'll lay my last dollar bill he'll come home with one heck of a great salmon.

GENERAL. Mac's a mighty good ghillie, I know, but he can't conjure up a fish at the touch of his wand—or should I say gaff.

LARRY. But Mac's uncle can.

GENERAL. Old Uncle Joe?

LARRY. That's him.

GENERAL. The one who got three months for poaching?

LARRY. Yes. Mac says he's lucky it wasn't six. (*He imitates Sam*) "A great day for salmon." (*He moves to the desk chair*) I don't mind betting that means he's bribed old Uncle Joe to go up to Lord whatever-his-name's water tonight, and net one for him.

GENERAL. Now, really! (*He rises*) I think that's going a bit far.

LARRY. Yes, maybe it is. Forget I ever said it.

GENERAL (*crossing to the trolley*) Have a drink?

LARRY. Thanks. (*He sits in the desk chair*)

GENERAL. What is it you like—Scotch on the rocks?

LARRY. Not too heavy.

(*The* GENERAL *pours two drinks*)

You know, Colonel, this is really quite a place.

GENERAL. I couldn't agree more.

LARRY. Central heating—servants galore—every comfort——

(*The* GENERAL *hands a drink to Larry*)

—drinks on the house—best steaks in Europe—fishing at the bottom of the garden . . .

GENERAL. I agree. I always stay here myself whenever I can.

LARRY (*rising and raising his glass*) Good luck, sir.

GENERAL. Good health. (*He crosses with his drink towards the fireplace*)

LARRY. Colonel, would you mind if I asked you something?

GENERAL (*stopping and turning*) Go ahead.

LARRY. Something sort of personal.

GENERAL. What about?

LARRY. About this place. This set-up.

GENERAL (*anxiously*) No—no, of course not.

LARRY (*moving to* L *of the General*) Your sister-in-law—Mrs Fitz-adam. A mighty fine woman, if I may say so.

GENERAL. I'm glad you think so.

LARRY (*crossing down* R) The way she runs this place. Why, she might have been in the hotel business all her life.

GENERAL. You must tell her.

LARRY (*turning to him*) The way she makes you feel you're one of the family.

GENERAL. I often feel that myself. (*He drinks*)

LARRY. But it isn't just her ability. (*He moves to* R *of the sofa*) It's her enthusiasm. The way she's always so cheerful. Never gives in.

GENERAL. Gives in?

LARRY. When you think of the tragedy of her husband's death— (*he moves and puts his glass on the mantelpiece*) one moment hale and hearty—a fine husband, no doubt—then suddenly—poof, and he's gone.

GENERAL. Too bad.

LARRY. What a terrible shock for her.

GENERAL. Terrible. (*He drains his glass*) Have another drink?

LARRY. No, thanks. I still have some.

GENERAL (*crossing to the trolley*) If you don't mind, I will. (*He refills his glass*)

LARRY (*moving to* R *of the sofa*) Colonel, you've got to help me. I'm just crazy about Dodo.

GENERAL. Most people are.

LARRY. But I mean—stark, staring crazy—head over heels in love with her. I want to marry her.

GENERAL (*turning*) Good God!

LARRY. Funny sort of nature she's got. If you didn't know what she'd been through, you might even think she was kind of cold.

GENERAL (*moving to* L *of the sofa*) Would you now?

LARRY. Not that we're well acquainted yet. (*He moves to the fire-place*) I've only kissed her twice.

GENERAL. Only twice? Did she—respond?

LARRY (*turning to him*) That's the whole trouble. You know how it is, Colonel, when you kiss a girl—a girl who has really given you the green light?

GENERAL. You mean the go?

LARRY. How all the forces of nature suddenly get galvanized into action. How all the allergies automatically act in unison—how all the chemistries start charging—and spark off the vibrations?

GENERAL (*sitting on the sofa at the left end*) Good Heavens!

LARRY (*sitting on the sofa at the right end*) You know what I mean?

GENERAL (*anxiously*) And so far Dodo hasn't vibrated?

LARRY. As I said. That's the whole trouble. But my God, she will. And that's where you can help.

GENERAL (*aghast*) Me?
LARRY (*leaning towards him*) You've got to sell me like I was the greatest bill of goods you've ever handled.

(LADY FITZADAM *enters up* C.
    PRAWN *follows her on*)

LADY FITZADAM (*as she enters*) I do hope you enjoyed your supper.
PRAWN (*closing the doors*) Delicious, thank you.
LADY FITZADAM (*moving down* C) Now, come and meet my brother-in-law.

(LARRY *and the* GENERAL *rise.* LARRY *moves to the fireplace.* PRAWN *crosses below Lady Fitzadam and shakes hands with the General*)

PRAWN. Very glad to meet you.
GENERAL. How are you?
PRAWN. All the better for a delicious meal. In fact, I don't think that outside of London, of course, I don't think I can ever remember . . .

(LARRY *realizes he knows Prawn and crosses below the General to* R *of Prawn*)

LARRY. The Prawn! (*He shakes Prawn violently by the hand*)
PRAWN (*responding enthusiastically*) Larry!
GENERAL (*moving down* R) You two know each other?
LARRY. Know each other? I'll say! Why, the times we had together in California. (*He slaps Prawn on the back*)

(LADY FITZADAM *moves to* L *of the table down* L)

(*He turns to the General*) Now here's a guy with all the answers—what he doesn't know about vibrations . . .
LADY FITZADAM. Vibrations?
GENERAL. We were discussing biological chemistry.
LARRY. Now, I ask you, Colonel—look at the Prawn. Would you say he was a lady-killer?
PRAWN (*crossing below Larry to* R *of him*) That's quite enough of that.

(LADY FITZADAM *crosses to* L *of Larry*)

LARRY. You keep quiet. I'm telling you, Colonel. This guy is dynamite. The first time we met was in the dining-car on the Santa Fé—(*to Prawn*) remember?
PRAWN. I'll never forget it.
LARRY. Funny-looking guy, I thought. No-one but a Limey could wear a mustash like that—and he'd have to be a Dook. Then d'you know what happened?
GENERAL. No.
LARRY. A dame walks by . . .
LADY FITZADAM. Yes?

LARRY. She took one look at the Prawn and fell flat on her face.
PRAWN. You mustn't believe a word of it.
LARRY. Just lay there panting. It was the same all over Cali-
fornia. They went down like ninepins. You see what I mean,
Colonel? Vibrations!
LADY FITZADAM (*crossing below Larry to* L *of Prawn*) And to think
I brought you two together.
PRAWN. You did?
LADY FITZADAM. All my fault, I'm afraid. We—that is, I—opened
a letter meant for you—rang up to explain that I didn't know where
you were—and here they are.
PRAWN. They?

(LADY FITZADAM *moves to* R *of Larry*)

So you came with the little bloke in glasses—the one I met in the
jewellers?

(LADY FITZADAM *sits on the sofa at the left end*)

LARRY. He's my pal.
PRAWN. Then I trust you're being as lucky as he is.
LARRY. Fishing?
PRAWN (*shaking his head*) The ladies—God bless 'em!
LARRY. How come?
PRAWN. If what he was paying for those brooches was anything
to go by . . . (*He turns suddenly to Lady Fitzadam*) Has he brought you
any presents yet?
LADY FITZADAM. Mr Goulansky?
PRAWN. No—Larry.

(*The* GENERAL *moves to* R *of the sofa.* LARRY *moves down* LC)

LADY FITZADAM. Of course not.
PRAWN (*moving slightly towards Larry*) You've got to watch these
Americans, Mrs Fitzadam. No holding 'em once they get on the
trail.

(LARRY *sits on the chair below the table down* L)

(*He crosses to the General*) Just as well you're here, Colonel, to act as
chaperone.
GENERAL. Yes, perhaps you're right.
LADY FITZADAM. Have you been in Scotland long?
PRAWN (*turning to her*) Been sailing up the west coast. Dropped
in to see Bunny Appleby. (*He sits on the sofa at the right end*) Know
him?
LADY FITZADAM. Lord Appleby? Yes.
GENERAL (*sitting on the firestool*) Do any fishing?
PRAWN. No time. Been terribly busy, I'm afraid. Not that
there'd have been much point.
GENERAL. But why?

(*The* CORPORAL *enters up* C, *carrying a tray with sandwiches.* LADY FITZADAM *rises, moves to the Corporal and looks as though giving him instructions in a whisper*)

PRAWN. Poor old Bunny. One of the worst seasons they've ever had.

LADY FITZADAM. Thank you, Mr Green.

GENERAL (*to Prawn*) What's the trouble? Not enough water?

PRAWN. Poaching!

(LADY FITZADAM *and the* CORPORAL *freeze*)

GENERAL. Poaching?

PRAWN. Kid in a Boy Scout camp swears he saw him.

GENERAL. The poacher?

PRAWN. A few nights ago—nets, gaffs, the lot. Poor old Bunny. I thought he was going to have a stroke. Never heard such language —ladies present, too. Swore blue murder and then rang up the Air Force to borrow police dogs.

(*The* CORPORAL *moves to the downstage end of the table down* L)

LADY FITZADAM (*moving to* L *of the sofa*) Alsatians?

PRAWN. And the military for some gelignite.

LARRY (*rising*) But that's lethal. (*He crosses and sits on the stool* C)

PRAWN. Maybe it is, but Bunny's a law unto himself. Spent all yesterday laying booby traps round his best pools.

LARRY. High explosives?

PRAWN. Rather clever, I thought. Rammed the lumps of gelignite into his old socks, made a hole in the toe—those that hadn't got holes already—then connected up to an electric trip wire.

LARRY. That's worse than the Klu Klux Klan.

PRAWN. Must say I thought it was a bit overdoing it myself. But that's Bunny all over. Enough explosives to wipe out a regiment.

(*The* CORPORAL *finds this too much. He drops the sandwich tray with a clatter, spilling the sandwiches on the floor. He immediately picks up the tray and dashes out up* C)

Anything wrong?

LADY FITZADAM (*moving to the table behind the sofa*) No, no—nothing at all. (*She picks up a box of cigarettes and offers it to Prawn*) Cigarette?

PRAWN. No, thanks—never use 'em.

LADY FITZADAM. I know—a cigar? (*She replaces the box and moves up* C)

(*The* GENERAL *puts his glass on the table* RC)

PRAWN. That I must admit would be the crowning glory to a perfect meal.

GENERAL (*rising*) I'll get 'em. (*He crosses to* L *of the sofa*)

LADY FITZADAM (*playing her part*) Do you know where they are kept?

E

GENERAL (*forgetting his part*) Well, of course I . . .

(LADY FITZADAM *makes frantic signs to the General*)

In the same place as the last time I came to stay—when I was staying here the last time.

LADY FITZADAM. How clever of you to remember.

(*The* GENERAL *exits up* R, *closing the door behind him.* PRAWN *rises, moves down* R *and looks at the picture.* LADY FITZADAM *moves below the left end of the sofa.* LARRY *rises and tries to kiss her*)

LARRY (*sotto voce*) You're adorable.

LADY FITZADAM (*sotto voce*) Larry, please. (*She pushes him away and sits* C *of the sofa*)

(*The* CORPORAL *enters up* C, *carrying a dustpan and brush. He moves down* LC. LARRY *crosses to the upstage french windows and goes on to the terrace.*

SAM *enters by the downstage french windows*)

SAM (*to the Corporal*) Where's Suzie?

CORPORAL. Washing up. Got to take her turn with the rest.

SAM. But it's a full moon.

CORPORAL. It's a full sink. (*He goes on to his knees and sweeps up the sandwiches*)

LADY FITZADAM. Ah, Mr Goulansky. Here's Mr Vernon, to whom you so kindly recommended us.

(SAM *crosses and shakes hands with Prawn*)

SAM. Nice to see you again. Glad you took my advice. You won't regret it.

PRAWN. I'm quite sure of that.

(LARRY *comes in by the downstage french windows and moves to the armchair* LC)

LARRY. How come this Vernon tally? You used to be Fuchs. And you were so high that night in California you spelt it with a double F.

(*The* CORPORAL *rises and exits with the dustpan and brush up* R)

PRAWN (*crossing to* R *of Larry*) It was a couple of F's Ffoulkes before I sold this place—before my uncle died, and I inherited the title.

LARRY. The title?

PRAWN (*moving to* L *of Sam*) When I became Lord Vernon.

LARRY. You're a lord?

LADY FITZADAM. Lord Vernon. Now where have I heard that name before?

PRAWN (*moving below the right end of the sofa*) It gets bandied about in the Press quite a lot. That's why I always drop the lord when—

as you might say—off duty. Stops people pointing and staring. So I'd be most grateful if when my wife arrives . . .

LADY FITZADAM (*rising*) I've got it.

PRAWN. What?

LADY FITZADAM. Didn't you marry Caroline Bruce?

PRAWN. Do you know her?

LADY FITZADAM. She was left half to my wing at Roedean.

PRAWN. Have you seen her lately?

LADY FITZADAM. Not since then. (*She moves up* c) I wonder if I've still got it?

SAM. What?

LADY FITZADAM. A hockey group. Taken just after we'd beaten Sherborne. Caroline fed me the winning goal. I must find it.

(LADY FITZADAM *exits up* c. PRAWN *starts to follow her but is stopped by* LARRY)

LARRY. Jees, I just can't get over this. There you were beating it up in the red woods—the terror of every striptease in California —The Amorous Prawn.

(*The* CORPORAL *enters up* R. *He carries his dustpan and brush, now empty*)

And here you are now—married to a hockey captain.

(*The telephone rings. The* CORPORAL *goes to the telephone and lifts the receiver, juggling with the dustpan which gets in the way. He uses a pseudo suave voice, which he adopts for these occasions.* SAM *sits on the footstool*)

CORPORAL (*into the telephone*) Glenmally House—Reception . . . (*His expression changes*) War Office? . . .

(PRAWN *crosses to the telephone*)

Sorry, chum, you've got the wrong number.

PRAWN (*taking the receiver*) Mine, I think. (*Into the telephone*) War Office? . . . Duty officer, please . . . Thanks . . . That the duty officer? . . . Secretary of State for War here . . .

(LARRY *and* SAM *look tremendously impressed.* LARRY *moves below the left end of the sofa. The* CORPORAL *looks horror-struck and backs above the sofa*)

Get hold of one of my private secretaries, will you? (*He sits on the sofa at the right end*) Tell him I shan't be back for a couple of days— going to do one or two surprise inspections . . . Yes, that's right. Tell him to explain to the P.M. about Thursday's Cabinet meeting . . . And, by the way—North-Western District must be around here somewhere. Find out, will you? I'd like to call on the G.O.C. I'm at—(*he looks at the telephone*) Glenmally one-o . . .

(*The* CORPORAL *edges to the door up* R)

Oh, and ask my private secretary to ring my flat. He'll know the form. You'll call me back? . . . That's right—Glenmally one-o. (*He replaces the receiver and looks around, pleased at the impression his conversation has made on the Americans*)

LARRY. You mean to say that you're the Secretary of State for War?

SAM (*rising*) You don't say!

PRAWN (*pompously*) If you want to get on in life, marry the head man's daughter. If he hasn't a daughter, marry his niece. I married the Prime Minister's—after that I couldn't go wrong.

SAM. Now, Larry, that's the way to do it. (*He crosses to the armchair* LC *and sits*)

> (LARRY *sits on the sofa at the left end.*
> *The* GENERAL *enters up* R, *carrying a box of cigars*)

GENERAL. Sorry I've been so long.

> (*The* CORPORAL *grabs the General by the arm and whispers the ghastly news*)

(*He refuses to take the Corporal seriously and laughs*) What? Don't be silly. (*He moves below the sofa and offers the cigars to Larry*) The big ones looked a bit mildewy and I couldn't find the others.

> (LARRY *refuses*)

(*He offers the box to Prawn*) I'd try one of these.

PRAWN (*taking a cigar*) Thanks very much. (*He lights his cigar with matches from the table* RC)

GENERAL (*crossing to Sam*) Mr Goulansky?

SAM (*taking a cigar*) Thanks. (*He puts the cigar in his pocket*) I'll smoke it later.

PRAWN. Tell me, Colonel, when did you retire?

GENERAL (*crossing to the desk*) Me—retire? Oh, it must be a good six years now.

PRAWN. And who was head man then?

GENERAL (*putting the box of cigars on the desk*) C.I.G.S.?

PRAWN. No, no. War Minister?

GENERAL. Let me think. Ah, yes. Mossy Maitland.

PRAWN. Ah—Mossy. Not too popular, I believe.

GENERAL (*moving slightly* C) Mossy? Just about the most popular War Minister we've ever had.

> (*The* CORPORAL *desperately tries from behind Prawn's back to signal the identity of Prawn, but the* GENERAL *ignores him*)

PRAWN. But surely a Labour . . . ?

GENERAL. Labour be damned! The Army's not interested in politics.

> (*The* CORPORAL *takes a box of matches from his pocket and crosses to the General*)

Interested in people who know their job.

(*The* CORPORAL *strikes a match in the General's face in an attempt to get him to pay attention to what he is trying to tell him*)

What's this for? Go away!

(*The* CORPORAL *throws the spent match out of the downstage window and crosses to the trolley*)

Take Mossy. Private in the first war—won a D.C.M. Got his commission on his own merit. Went into politics and fought his way to the top. Guts. Guts—bags of guts.

PRAWN. Quite, quite. But apart from the purely physical aspect . . .

(*The* CORPORAL *knocks two bottles together to attract the General's attention, but fails to do so*)

GENERAL (*moving to* L *of the sofa*) Physical, my backside! Look at the poops they've got hanging around Whitehall today.

(LARRY *tries to rise to intervene*)

LARRY. Colonel, I don't think you realize . . .

GENERAL (*pushing Larry back on to his seat*) You keep out of this, you don't understand. (*He moves* C)

PRAWN (*rising and crossing to* R *of the General*) Perhaps I should explain, Colonel . . .

GENERAL (*warming up*) Look at 'em. Experience—my aunt Fanny. All that matters today is influence—got to be one of the family——

(*The* CORPORAL *rocks the chair down* L *backwards and forwards in a final attempt to distract the General*)

—that or have a handle to your name.

(*The* CORPORAL'S *frantic signals have now become too much for the* GENERAL)

(*He swings round on the Corporal*) What's the matter with you, Corporal?

PRAWN. Corporal?

(*The* GENERAL *realizes his blunder and covers up*)

GENERAL. In his spare time, Mr Green is a Territorial. (*He is rather pleased with this and crosses below Prawn to the fireplace*)

PRAWN (*immediately the politician*) A Territorial? You belong to a great force, Mr Green; one with a noble and gallant tradition. In these days of high taxation and reduced Service estimates—we must rely more and more on the patriotism of the citizen Army— in fact, our Territorials. (*He holds out his hand*)

(*The* CORPORAL *moves slowly to Prawn and shakes hands, wondering what will happen next*)

I'm proud to know you, Corporal Green.

(*The* GENERAL *moves above the sofa*)

SAM (*to Larry*) At home that speech would win an election.

(*The telephone rings*)

PRAWN. See who it is, Corporal.

(*The telephone rings. The* CORPORAL *has no alternative but to answer it. He crosses to the telephone, gingerly lifts the receiver and winces when he hears "War Office" from the caller*)

GENERAL. Well—who's it for?

CORPORAL (*miserably*) The Secretary of State for War.

(PRAWN *crosses and takes the receiver. The* CORPORAL *joins the* GENERAL *on whom the truth is dawning*)

PRAWN (*into the telephone*) Speaking . . . Well done . . . P.M. quite happy? . . . Good . . . Good . . . You rang the flat? . . .

(SAM *rises, crosses to the trolley and pours himself a drink*)

Good . . . Good . . . What's that? . . . (*He sits on the sofa at the right end*) I asked you to find out the telephone number of the official residence of the General Officer Commanding North-Western District, not the telephone number of the place where I'm staying . . . (*Scathingly*) It may interest you to know that even Cabinet Ministers are capable of reading the number on a dial. And this dial reads very distinctly "Glenmally one-o" . . .

(*The* GENERAL *crosses and sinks into the desk chair*)

I don't give a damn what the exchange say . . . Ring up the Postmaster-General. All I want to know is where I can get in touch with the General Officer Commanding North-Western District. (*He slams down the receiver, rises, crosses to the fireplace, removes his spectacles and puts them on the mantelpiece*) Can you beat it? All I want is a straightforward answer to a straightforward question.

LARRY (*laughing*) It never failed with the girls in California.

PRAWN. There's going to be some sweeping changes in the Army before I'm much older.

SAM. That's what we could do with at the Pentagon. The place is packed with racketeers. Every one making something on the side.

(LADY FITZADAM *enters up* C, *carrying a photograph album*)

LADY FITZADAM (*moving down* C) I've found it.

PRAWN (*crossing to* R *of Lady Fitzadam*) Let's have a look.

LADY FITZADAM. I bet you can't tell which is Caroline.

LARRY (*rising and moving to* R *of Prawn*) I bet I can find Dodo—I mean—our madam.

(SAM *goes on to the terrace by the downstage french windows*)
LADY FITZADAM. I'll give you three goes.
LARRY (*pointing*) That one.
LADY FITZADAM. Wrong.
LARRY (*pointing*) There—with a fringe.
LADY FITZADAM. Wrong again.

(*The baying of Alsatians is heard off in the distance.*
SAM *comes in by the upstage french windows*)

PRAWN (*crossing to the fireplace*) Alsatians!

(*The others look round, horrified. There is a pause then a very loud explosion is heard, followed immediately by red flashes in the sky. The baying of the dogs grows louder*)

LARRY. My God!
GENERAL. Booby traps? More like a land mine.

(*The* CORPORAL *crosses to the trolley and pours a drink which he hands to the General*)

CORPORAL. Poor old Joe.
LARRY (*moving to* R *of the sofa*) But this is murder. Stark murder!
PRAWN. Whatever it is, I bet Bunny won't have any more poachers for a while.
LARRY. Talk about gangsters!
PRAWN. I'll ring him in the morning and find out what happened.

(LADY FITZADAM *moves to the armchair* LC)

SAM (*moving* LC) Why not call him now?
PRAWN (*moving below the left end of the sofa*) What's the good? The house is at least a couple of miles from the river. Anyhow, they won't dare to make a search before daylight—dangerous place, a river bank in the dark.
SAM. I'll say. (*He goes on to the terrace by the upstage french windows*)
LADY FITZADAM (*sitting in the armchair*) I feel rather faint.

(*The* GENERAL *rises and moves to Lady Fitzadam. The* CORPORAL *goes to the trolley and pours a drink for Lady Fitzadam*)

LARRY (*crossing to the trolley*) Let me get you a drink—a little brandy? (*He takes the drink from the Corporal and hands it to Lady Fitzadam*)
LADY FITZADAM. Thanks.

(PRAWN *resumes his conversation with the* GENERAL *who now comes to attention in deference to the Minister*)

PRAWN. Colonel. Coming back to Mossy Maitland. All very well

for him to write letters to *The Times* accusing the War Office of red
tape—pure political vote-catching.

(LADY FITZADAM, *slightly flushed by the brandy, slams her glass on to
the table down* L)

LADY FITZADAM. Good old Mossy!
PRAWN (*taken aback*) I beg your pardon?

(*The* GENERAL *makes signs to silence* LADY FITZADAM *who dis-
regards his signals*)

LADY FITZADAM. Anyone who stirs up that damned War Office
deserves every possible encouragement.
PRAWN (*turning to the fireplace*) Well, really!
GENERAL. Dodo, please.

(LADY FITZADAM *rises, moves to the desk and takes a War Office
letter from under the blotter*)

LADY FITZADAM. I bet no American General would stand for this.
PRAWN (*turning*) For what?

(SAM *comes in by the upstage french windows.* LARRY *moves below
the desk. The* GENERAL *sits in the desk chair*)

LADY FITZADAM (*crossing to* C) This letter. Written to—a great
friend of mine. A man who'd served his country for over forty years.
PRAWN. Army?
LADY FITZADAM (*nodding*) Over forty years. Two World Wars and
heaven knows how many campaigns in between.
PRAWN. What's his name?
LADY FITZADAM. No, I promised I wouldn't tell. Wounded twice,
nearly killed I don't know how many times. And what happens
when he reaches the end of his service—and it's time to retire?

(*The* GENERAL *buries his head in his hands*)

Some podgy little politician—a man who's never seen action in his
life—never got nearer to being wounded than wearing out the seat
of his pants——
SAM (*moving above the left end of the sofa*) Atta-girl, Sister.
LADY FITZADAM. —has the audacity, the damned cheek to . . .

(*The sound of drunken singing is heard off* L)

What's that?
CORPORAL. I'll deal with him. (*He dashes out of the downstage french
windows and along the terrace*)

(HUGGINS *enters very unsteadily by the upstage french windows before
the* CORPORAL *can reach him.* HUGGINS *wears his uniform*)

HUGGINS. Evening, all.

(SAM *pulls Huggins up* C)

SAM. Are you another Territorial? Tell you what, Huggins—I got a swell idea. How about giving us "Gunga Din"? I'll get the props.

(SAM *exits up* C. HUGGINS' *eyes light up at the thought of giving a performance*)

HUGGINS. It'll cost you time and a half after ten o'clock.
LARRY (*moving to Huggins*) Be a pal, Huggins. (*To the others*) This is really something, folks. Come on, Huggins, please. (*He takes a pound note from his pocket and gives it to Huggins*) Y'know, he's a real busker. Won't work without his money.

(SAM *enters up* C, *carrying the General's cap. The* GENERAL *sees this but is unable to stop it and buries his head in his arms on the desk.* LARRY *crosses and sits on the chair down* L. SAM *gives the cap to Huggins and stands above the sofa. The* CORPORAL *stands by the trolley*)

SAM. It's all yours, Huggins. Ladies and Gentlemen—"Gunga Din".

(HUGGINS *takes a deep breath and moves* C)

HUGGINS. "If", by Rudyard Kipling. (*With each exhortation, he lunges towards a member of his audience, starting with Sam*)
   "*If* you can keep your head when all about you are
         losing theirs and blaming it on you,
(*To Larry*)
   If you can trust yourself when all men doubt you
   Yet make allowance for their doubting, too.
(*He crosses to Prawn*)
   If you can dream and not make dreams your master,
(*He puts his hand on Prawn's shoulder and pushes him down on to the fire-stool*)
   If you can think and not make thoughts your aim,
(*He crosses to* R *of the General*)
   If you can meet with triumph and disaster
   And treat those two impostors just the same.
(*He puts a hand on the General's shoulder and pulls him back in the chair*)
   If you can bear to hear the truth you've spoken,
   Twisted by knaves to make a trap for fools.

(*The* GENERAL *slowly rises*)

   Or see the things you gave your life for, broken
   And stoop and build them up again with worn-out tools.

   If you can make one heap of all your winnings . . ."

(*He recognizes the General. His voice dies away and he suddenly springs to attention with a tremendous click of heels*) Sir!

PRAWN (*rising*) Who is this?

HUGGINS. Three-two-eight-four-o-four Private Huggins, sir. (*He dives a hand into his trousers pocket, fishes out a cablegram and hands it to the General*) Cable, sir.

(*The* GENERAL *snatches the cable and throws it on to the desk. The telephone rings. The* GENERAL *crosses to the telephone, but* PRAWN *gets there first*)

PRAWN. Mine, I think.

(*The telephone rings.* SAM *moves to* R *of Huggins*)

SAM. You slayed 'em, Huggins.

(*The* CORPORAL *moves to Huggins.* PRAWN *lifts the receiver*)

CORPORAL. He's in enough trouble as it is. (*To Huggins*) About turn. Quick march. Left, right . . .

(HUGGINS *marches off up* C.
The CORPORAL *follows him off.*
SAM *follows the Corporal off, closing the doors behind him. The* GENERAL *crosses to the desk chair and sits*)

PRAWN (*into the telephone*) Secretary of State, speaking . . .

(LADY FITZADAM *reacts, crosses to the General and puts her arm on his shoulder to comfort him*)

Put him through . . . That the duty officer? . . . You've checked up and I am speaking from the residence . . .

(LADY FITZADAM *crosses and stands above the sofa*)

Yes, I'm beginning to think you're right . . May seem extraordinary to you, Major, but not half so extraordinary as it seems to me. And who is the G.O.C.? . . .

(BIDDY *enters up* C, *moves to* L *of Lady Fitzadam and whispers to her.* LADY FITZADAM *signals Biddy to tell her later*)

Sir Hamish Fitzadam? . . . Thank you very much. (*He replaces the receiver*)

(BIDDY *whispers to Lady Fitzadam then exits up* C, *leaving the door open*)

(*He moves below the sofa and addresses the General*) Perhaps we'd better have a quiet chat, General.

GENERAL (*rising*) Care to come along to my study, sir?

LADY FITZADAM (*moving to* L *of the sofa*) Your wife has arrived and gone straight to her room. I'll make sure she's got everything she wants. (*She turns to go*)
PRAWN (*quickly*) Don't worry.

(LADY FITZADAM *stops and turns*)

I expect she's dead tired. (*To the General*) On second thoughts, probably more regular if I said what I have to say in writing. I'll communicate from London. (*He crosses to Lady Fitzadam*)
GENERAL. As you wish, sir.
PRAWN (*to Lady Fitzadam*) My wife and I will be off early in the morning. Don't bother to come down. (*He crosses to Larry*) So long, Larry.
LARRY (*rising and shaking hands*) So long, Prawny.
PRAWN. Look me up in Whitehall sometime.
LARRY. I'll do that.
PRAWN (*moving to Lady Fitzadam*) Oh, my bill. Perhaps you'll send it to the War Office.

(PRAWN *exits up* C, *leaving the doors open. The* GENERAL *sits in the desk chair.* LARRY *stands looking out of the downstage french windows*)

LADY FITZADAM (*moving to the General*) All my fault, darling.
GENERAL. Just as much mine as yours.
LARRY (*moving to the downstage end of the desk*) Let's get this straight. Hamish isn't your brother-in-law at all. He's your husband and this is his official residence.
LADY FITZADAM. An awful lot of lies, I'm afraid, but they were in such a good cause that it made them seem almost white.

(*The* CORPORAL *and* SUZIE *enter up* C *and move to* L *of the sofa.* SUZIE *is* R *of the Corporal*)

CORPORAL. If I may say so—and on behalf of all the staff, may I say how sorry we all are, and that no matter what happens, we're right behind you, madam—my lady.
LADY FITZADAM. Thank you, Mr Green—Corporal. Oh, dear, I'm in such a muddle I don't know where I am.
GENERAL. What we all need is a good stiff drink.
LARRY. You're telling me.
GENERAL. And that goes for you, too, Corporal, and you, too, Suzie.
CORPORAL. Thank you, sir.

(SUZIE *crosses to the trolley. The* CORPORAL *follows her.* SUZIE *removes her brooches and gives them to the Corporal*)

LADY FITZADAM (*sitting on the sofa at the right end*) Larry.

(LARRY *crosses to* L *of the sofa. The* CORPORAL *pours the drinks*)

When I telephoned you at the *Savoy*, well, it just seemed too good an opportunity to miss. You wanting to come to Scotland to fish, and we needing the money so badly for our new home, the one where we're going to retire. It all sounded too good to be true.

LARRY. Sam and I should worry. We've had a wonderful time, wonderful food . . .

(*The* GENERAL *rises, crosses to Lady Fitzadam and takes his bridge winnings from his pocket*)

GENERAL. My humble contribution. (*He hands the notes to Lady Fitzadam*)

(LARRY *crosses to* LC)

LADY FITZADAM (*rising and counting the notes*) Your bridge winnings? Thank heaven there's something we've made on the level.

(PRAWN *enters up* C *and crosses to the fireplace*)

PRAWN (*looking at the notes*) Stocktaking? Must have left my glasses behind. (*He collects his spectacles from the mantelpiece*) Ah, here they are.

(*A piercing female scream is heard off*)

LARRY (*facing up* C) It's Sam.
LADY FITZADAM (*crossing down* C) Where's Suzie?
CORPORAL (*stepping aside*) I've got her here.

(SUZIE *moves above the table down* L)

SUZIE. And Biddy's out in the garden with Willie.
LADY FITZADAM (*turning to Prawn*) Then that only leaves your wife.
PRAWN. What?

(PRAWN *runs off up* C)

LARRY. It's pathological.

(LARRY *runs off up* C. *The* CORPORAL *picks up a tray with two drinks and moves* LC. *The* GENERAL *sits* C *of the sofa*)

GENERAL (*striking off with his fingers*) Using an official residence for financial gain. Encouraging drunk and disorderly conduct amongst the other ranks. Insulting a Cabinet Minister. Allowing his wife to be . . . (*He holds out his hand to Lady Fitzadam*)

(LADY FITZADAM *moves and sits* L *of the General on the sofa*)

I wonder what the official term for that is?
LADY FITZADAM. "Caught in a pincer movement", any good?

(*The* CORPORAL *crosses with the drinks to the sofa*)

(*She takes a glass*) Thank you, Corporal. (*She hands the glass to the General and takes a drink for herself*)

GENERAL. Thank you, Mr Green.

(LARRY *enters up* C *holding an indignant* SAM *by the collar.* LARRY *brings him down* C *and drops him to the floor*)

LARRY. You get right down on your knees and apologize.

SAM. Apologize?

LARRY. Making passes at Lord Vernon's wife.

SAM. She's not his wife.

(*The* GENERAL *and* LADY FITZADAM *rise*)

GENERAL. Not his wife?

SAM. Are you kidding? That's Babs.

LARRY. Babs?

SAM (*rising*) From Oban. She's the barmaid at the *Red Lion*.

GENERAL (*overjoyed*) The Secretary of State for War at North-Western District Headquarters with a barmaid. That's just what the Opposition are praying for.

LADY FITZADAM. Now we've got the Prawn where we want him. Sam—I could hug you.

SAM. You could? (*He advances on Lady Fitzadam*)

LARRY (*pulling Sam* L) You stay right here.

(PRAWN *enters up* C *and moves to* L *of the sofa*)

PRAWN. Could I see that letter?

LADY FITZADAM. The one from the War Office? (*She picks up the letter from the sofa, and hands it to Prawn*)

(PRAWN *reads the letter then tears it up*)

PRAWN. On second thoughts, perhaps we'd better tear this up. I'll see that the necessary transport is arranged.

GENERAL (*bitingly*) How very considerate of you, sir. (*He splutters into his drink*)

CORPORAL (*moving to* R *of Prawn*) Perhaps his lordship would give her ladyship the cheque for the Zardeens.

PRAWN. Oh, yes. How much?

CORPORAL. Five at seventy pounds. Three hundred and fifty quid.

PRAWN. But you said sixty-five.

CORPORAL. They've gone up.

(*The baying of the Alsatians in full cry and rapidly approaching is heard*)

LADY FITZADAM. Alsatians!

(*The* CORPORAL *rushes to the upstage french windows and looks out*)

CORPORAL. It's Uncle Joe. He's all right.

UNCLE JOE *staggers in by the upstage french windows. He is in oilskins and waders. He closes the windows behind him and moves down* C. PRAWN *moves above the sofa.* SUZIE *closes the downstage french windows. The* CORPORAL *stands by the desk chair.* UNCLE JOE *opens his coat and produces an enormous salmon.* SAM *and* LARRY *produce pound notes and bargain with* UNCLE JOE *for the salmon.* LARRY *pushes* SAM *into the armchair and the* GENERAL *takes* LADY FITZADAM *in his arms as—*

the CURTAIN *falls*

FURNITURE AND PROPERTY LIST

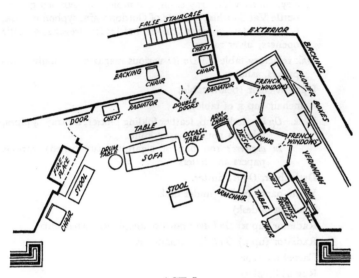

ACT I

On stage: Oak high-backed chair (down R)

Long, upholstered firestool

On mantelpiece: clock, ashtray, ornaments, invitation card

In fireplace: firegrate, fire-irons, firescreen

Over fireplace: electric wall-brackets, large oil paint of "Hunter and Dog", large antlers

Small drum table (R of sofa) *On it:* telephone, desk bell-push, message-pad, ashtray

    Under it: Lady Fitzadam's black shoes

Sofa. *On it:* cushions, copy of *Sporting Life*

    Over back of sofa: Lady Fitzadam's jacket and belt

Occasional table (L of sofa) *On it:* table-lighter, ashtray

Table (behind sofa) *On it:* 2 empty flower vases, tartan earmuffs wrapped in tissue paper, Lady Fitzadam's handbag, box of matches

Stool (down C) *On it:* copy of *Country Life* open at page showing "Gundog Manor", large round silver tray, large silver box of cigarettes, box of matches

Small maghogany chest (down L) *On it:* table-lamp, bowl of roses

On wall over chest down L: small gilt mirror

Small mahogany chest (up R) *On it:* table-lamp, ornament

Trolley. *On it:* white tray cloth, 4 tumblers, 8 stemmed glasses, bottle Vat 69 whisky, bottle of Gordon's gin, syphon of soda, 6 tonic waters, 3 bitter lemons, bottles for dressing, 3 bottle openers, silver salver

Oak refectory table (L) *On it:* various magazines, 3 daily newspapers, ashtray

Upright chair (below table)

Armchair (up R of table)

Desk. *On it:* desk lamp, leather folding blotter, ashtray, 4 pipes, tobacco pouch, paper knife

   In drawers: 100 box of cigarettes (unopened) various papers and letters

Desk chair. *On it:* duster

Waste-paper basket (under desk)

Chair (R of desk)

Radiator (up R) *On ledge:* bowl of anemones, ornaments

Radiator (up L) *On ledge:* ornaments

Carpet on floor

Rug at fireplace

Window curtains and pelmets

On window ledge down L: ashtray, ornament

On wall down R: shield with regimental motto, small modern painting

Over radiator up L: small modern painting

Over chest down L: small modern painting

On wall behind desk: 2 small modern paintings (1 not fixed permanently)

Over radiator up R: small antlers

Over double doors: large antlers

Over radiator up R, *under antlers:* oil painting of rural scene

In hall: 2 chairs
         small oak cupboard

On verandah: 2 boxes pink and white geraniums

Door up R closed

Double doors open

Upstage french windows closed

Downstage french windows open

Light fittings off

Off stage : Coins (SUZIE)
    2 small envelopes, stamped and addressed (SUZIE)
    Airmail letter, readdressed three times, containing Prawn's letter
    (SUZIE)
    Long white envelope, address typed, sealed and stamped containing letter from house agent (SUZIE)
    Trug basket. *In it :* bunch of sweet peas, bunch of stock, secateurs
    (LADY FITZADAM)
    Brief-case (GENERAL)
    Gardening gloves (LADY FITZADAM)
    General's overcoat (CORPORAL)
    General's hat, cane and gloves (HUGGINS)

Personal : LADY FITZADAM: handbag. *In it :* 5 £1 notes, pocket pencil, notebook
    CORPORAL: green baize apron, lighted cigarette, packet of
    Players cigarettes
    WILLIE: matches

ACT II

Strike : Desk chair
    All flowers
    Trug basket
    Gardening gloves
    Shoes
    Smock
    Newspapers
    Letters from desk
    Papers from desk
    Invitation card from mantelpiece
    Loose change
    Whisky bottle
    Gin bottle
    All glasses
    Empty tonic bottles, etc.

Set : *On table* R *of sofa :* scribbling pad and pencil
    On firestool : copy of *Country Life*
    Above stool C: tea trolley. *On it :* teapot, milk jug, slop basin, teacup,
    saucer, teaspoon, small plate and knife, silver muffin dish with
    lid, large plate with cake and knife

F

On radiator ledge up RC: bowl of yellow roses

On radiator ledge up L: vase of flowers

On window ledge down L: vase of flowers

On trolley down L: empty Haig whisky bottle, 6 large stemmed glasses, 3 whisky tumblers

On mantelpiece: cable envelope

On desk: inkstand and roller blotter

In firegrate: cashbox

Reverse desk and set against wall L

Set chair up LC at desk

Move desk lamp to downstage end of desk

Off stage: Account book (CORPORAL)

            Clipboard with paysheets (CORPORAL)

            4 pay packets, filled and sealed (CORPORAL)

            Bundle of 25 £1 notes (CORPORAL)

            2 £5 notes (CORPORAL)

            Fishing-rod and bag (LARRY)

            Tray. *On it:* bottle of whisky, bottle of gin, glass of whisky and ice, glass of gin and tonic (CORPORAL)

            Bundle of greenery (LARRY)

            Large army envelope. *In it:* letters (CORPORAL)

Personal: LADY FITZADAM: handbag

            SUZIE: 2 brooches

            SAM: £1 note

ACT III

Strike: Bundle of greenery

         Army envelope and letters

         Used glasses

         General's hat, cane and gloves

         Lady Fitzadam's handbag

Set: *On table* R *of sofa:* 2 coffee-cups, saucers and spoons

      On table L *of sofa:* 2 coffee-cups, saucers and spoons, large box of matches

      On table down L: silver tray with silver coffee-pot, milk jug and sugar basin

Army letter under blotter on desk
On table above sofa: cigarette box with cigarettes
On trolley: bowl with ice, bottle of brandy, clean glasses
On table L of sofa: ashtray
Doors closed
French windows open
Light fittings on
Window curtains open

Off stage: Ash collector (CORPORAL)
10 £1 notes (GENERAL)
Tray with sandwiches (CORPORAL)
Dustpan, brush (CORPORAL)
Box of cigars (GENERAL)
Photograph album (LADY FITZADAM)
General's cap (SAM)
Salmon (UNCLE JOE)

Personal: BIDDY: engagement ring
PRAWN: watch, notebook, spectacles, box with brooch
SAM: £1 notes
CORPORAL: matches
LARRY: £1 notes
HUGGINS: cablegram

LIGHTING PLOT

Property fittings required: 2 electric wall-brackets, 3-light desk lamp, 2 table-lamps

Interior. A living-room. The same scene throughout

THE APPARENT SOURCES OF LIGHT are in daytime, 2 french windows L, and a small window down L, and at night, wall-brackets over the mantelpiece R and table-lamps up R, L and down L

THE MAIN ACTING AREAS cover the whole stage

ACT I. A June morning

To open: Effect of bright sunshine
             Fittings off

No cues

ACT II. A June afternoon

To open: Effect of bright sunshine
             Fittings off

No cues

ACT III. Evening

To open: Fittings on
             Moonlight effect outside windows

No cues

EFFECTS PLOT

ACT I

Cue 1   At rise of CURTAIN   (Page 1)
Sounds from distant parade ground

Cue 2   SUZIE: "To Loch Lomond?"   (Page 3)
The telephone rings

Cue 3   LADY FITZADAM: ". . . Arms on it."   (Page 4)
Sound of car horn and sentries springing to attention

Cue 4   GENERAL: ". . . out so tidily."   (Page 5)
Telephone rings

Cue 5   The GENERAL exits   (Page 11)
Sounds of troops being brought to attention and a car driving away

Cue 6   CORPORAL: "Yes, madam."   (Page 20)
Telephone rings

ACT II

Cue 7   LARRY: ". . . I call her?"   (Page 34)
Telephone rings

Cue 8   GENERAL: ". . . you all right?"   (Page 41)
Telephone rings

Cue 9   GENERAL: ". . . felt quite sick."   (Page 45)
Telephone rings

ACT III

Cue 10   SUZIE: ". . . drink their health."   (Page 50)
Front-door bell rings

Cue 11   CORPORAL: ". . . offered me sixty."   (Page 52)
Telephone rings

Cue 12   LARRY: ". . . a hockey captain."   (Page 63)
Telephone rings

Cue 13   SAM: "... win an election."   (Page 66)
       Telephone rings

Cue 14   PRAWN: "... it is, Corporal."   (Page 66)
       Telephone rings

Cue 15   LADY FITZADAM: "Wrong again."   (Page 67)
       Baying of Alsatians

Cue 16   PRAWN: "Alsatians!"   (Page 67)
       Explosion and red flashes in sky. The baying grows louder

Cue 17   HUGGINS: "Cable, sir."   (Page 70)
       Telephone rings

Cue 18   PRAWN: "Mine, I think."   (Page 70)
       Telephone rings

Cue 19   CORPORAL: "They've gone up."   (Page 73)
       Baying of Alsatians

Lightning Source UK Ltd.
Milton Keynes UK
UKHW02f0957131217
314387UK00007B/793/P